Wendy   Merry.
         Christmas ·99

Read & enjoy! Beauty in
Simplicity. Life and living
with it's enjoyment need not
be complicated

Dad

NATURE DIARY OF A QUIET PEDESTRIAN

Nature Diary of a Quiet Pedestrian

Written and illustrated by Philip Croft

Foreword by Bob Switzer

Harbour Publishing
Madeira Park, BC

NATURE DIARY OF A QUIET PEDESTRIAN

Published by:
HARBOUR PUBLISHING CO. LTD.
P.O. Box 219, Madeira Park, BC Canada V0N 2H0

CANADIAN CATALOGUING IN PUBLICATION DATA

Croft, Philip.
    Nature diary of a quiet pedestrian

    Includes index.
    ISBN 0-920080-87-1

    1. Natural history – British Columbia – West Vancouver.
2. West Vancouver (B.C.) – Description.
I. Title.
QH106.2.B7C76 1986 508.711'33 C86-091502-6

Design by Gaye Hammond.
Printed in Hong Kong by Colorcraft Ltd.

Table of Contents

Foreword

It is a chilly, misty day in Sandy Cove, certainly not what one expects in July along our ocean front here in West Vancouver. Having just dumped a generous rain, the clouds are piled up against the North Shore mountains and the afternoon sky across the bay has a curious flat grayness. Yet I can see for miles to the southwest and the distant shapes of Vancouver Island.

My staunch little boat rides on its anchor against the tide. The coffee pot is on in the galley and I'm watching. There are no summer people on the beach. In fact, except for a couple of foraging seagulls, nature is still. My mind is flooded with memories and I feel as if I'm back at my little house on Rose Crescent just above the Cove.

For many years I would quietly descend the stone stairs from the road above, leaving the traffic noise, and enter the special world of the Cove where I could be a quiet onlooker, observing the myriad changes in nature which time and the seasons brought. I was and am a watcher.

Up the hill at the other end of our rather quaint, old-fashioned street lived Phil Croft, a man of senior years, quite small of build, neat and tidy, purposeful, with keen, alert eyes and a direct manner. And as I write this I can hear his enthusiastic voice. "How lovely! Isn't this a good day! Look how plump those blackberries are getting on the rocks above the beach. A few days of good hot sun and they'll be in a pie. But just smell that sea breeze. How fine!" Phil Croft was my neighbour and my friend and he was a walker.

In my den I have a painting he did looking out the Cove to the lighthouse. Every time I look at it I think of my friend and the lady who was his companion in life, Edith Croft. No man ever had a finer confidante or partner. She, within their small and lovely home perched on the granite bluff overlooking the ocean, provided the tranquil setting that these delightful people shared. She, listening with obvious pride and enjoyment to the recounting of Phil's morning ramble, and he, with undivided attention, receiving the latest news in the mail from the families of their son and daughter in Ontario. They adored their distant family, and if you were counted as a friend, you shared the intimacies of their lives. They loved their friends and shared a great joy in the world of nature. The little house on the bluff was always open to me and I would spend hours looking at botanical pictures and listening to the retelling of family adventures.

We travelled up into the mountains to the wildflower meadows and up the Sound to look at seals basking on the reefs. We had picnics and good dinners, and above all, good conversation. I miss my friends. They are both gone now, in fact within hours of one another. They lived to a high standard of service and dedication and in my heart I know I was greatly enriched by them. I like to remember that each day the walker returned to a hot cup of tea and a sharing of the adventure with his constant companion.

And it seems very proper that lovers of the outdoors will learn something of the wonders of nature from the legacy of watercolour paintings and the words in this book, carefully put down and illustrated, marking the passage of a year in one tiny corner of our huge country.

Bob Switzer

Preface

I am an inveterate pedestrian. I walk daily for pleasure, exercise and control of the waistline. But mostly for pleasure. For health of both body and mind there is nothing to beat pedestrianism. I suppose, since *pedis* in Latin means foot, any form of foot travel – running, leaping, or jogging (the current fad), might be classed as pedestrianism, but to me, Pedestrianism means walking. Walking has a long and honourable history. "When Israel came out of Egypt, the sea saw that and fled" – but Israel was walking. When Abraham came, by Divine command, out of his birthplace at Ur of the Chaldees and commenced his long trek to – wherever it was he was trekking to – he and his tribe were walking, or so we have been given to understand. So I, in my role as a Quiet Pedestrian, do not run, leap, or jog. I walk.

In my daily peregrinations I frequently pass, or rather am passed by, one or more earnestly persevering jogger, and I concede that when it is desirable to achieve a maximum of physical exercise in the shortest possible time, jogging must have something to recommend it. The determined and somewhat agonized expressions on the faces of these joggers assures me that they think so and are willing to take their chance on the possibility of foot problems and spine problems later in life in order to enjoy the more immediate health blessings that jogging is said to bestow.

But me, I like to walk. Moreover, I like to walk alone; I prefer to be a quiet pedestrian, to walk and think, not walk and converse. In this respect my hour afoot is apt to be the most useful and productive hour of my day, for it is a time during which I am able, to a measured footfall, to think many things through uninterruptedly, to a logical or practical conclusion. Have I a difficult letter to write, a difficult interview to face, an address to prepare, I do this planning best of all as a quiet, but by no means comatose pedestrian. It is my time for meditation and reflection.

During the nineteen forties, I came into possession of a number of very entertaining essays by a scholarly westernized Chinaman, Chiang-Yee, himself a quiet pedestrian, who wrote under the pseudonym of "The Silent Traveller." Like myself, Chiang-Yee liked to observe, and to draw and paint what he saw on his silent travels, though in his case it was the human pageant which captivated his pen and brush as he progressed, a silent traveller, in London, Oxford, Edinburgh, in the Yorkshire Dales, and in New York. Chiang, in his Edinburgh essay, points out that "silent traveller" is a "literary" translation of his Chinese nom-de-plume, Ya-hsin-chê, of which, however, a more exact and literal translation would be "dumb-walking-man."

Quiet Pedestrian. Silent Traveller. Dumb-walking-man.

To the many good people who, over the past fifteen years, have seen me pass along the residential streets and quiet by-ways which form my usual routes, often in inclement weather, politely but firmly declining kind offers of a lift from helpful motorists, "dumb-walking-man" might well seem the most apt of the three phrases.

But me, I like walking.

And then, too, there is the nature-watching. It is not necessary to travel to the out of the way wilderness areas of our province to be confronted with a year-long pageant of natural events in the life-cycles of common plants, insects, birds and animals. It is surprising how many species inhabit roadside ditches, patches of woodland, vacant lots, railway embankments and cuttings and similar waste spaces throughout our area. By following the same limited selection of routes day after day, week in and week out throughout the year, one is enabled to note every phase in the development of wild plants as they spring, grow, flower, seed and make their appearance; when the birds that feed on the insects appear and when they congregate for their annual migrations. This becomes a never-ending source of wonder and pleasure, which I hope these diary notes, and the water colours and line-drawings with which I have attempted to illustrate them, may in some small measure help to pass along to the reader.

Me, I like walking.

January

New Year's Day. The first day of January, of the year, and of the
new decade, the ninth of the ageing century. As I started out on my
regular "three-miler" I was confronted, this morning, by a landscape
made mysterious by a blanket of silvery sea fog which had settled
down during the night, a marine phenomenon of surprising beauty,
quite unlike the celebrated "pea-souper" of former days in London,
or the acrid petrol-induced miasma of industrial Los Angeles, but
instead, a cool, delicate vapourous covering that subtly alters the
entire appearance of the outdoor scene, softens outlines, and
produces a muting, not only of colours, but also of the sounds of
traffic from nearby Marine Drive. A magical world in which to walk
at leisure on a winter's morning.

Last night we "saw the New Year in," quietly, as is our custom. My
Constant Companion and I, sharing as we do a distaste for the
frantic merrymaking considered by many a necessary adjunct to
New Year's Eve, sat instead before a fire of glowing alder logs and
consoled and comforted the Old Year in its dying hours by recalling
with gratitude the happy, jolly, comfortable and memorable hours it
had brought us; there seemed no need to blow toy trumpets and
burst balloons. Our old grandfather clock, standing in the corner of
the hall, ticked his way with his customary solemnity, second by
second towards midnight, and, as he struck the hour, we opened the
French door to the patio overlooking the sea, and listened to a brief
hullabaloo as the scores of ships, anchored in the harbour and the
bay, but unseen in the fog, heralded the entry of AD 1981 with blasts
on their sirens. We "broke out" the decanter of port, and pledged
each other in that incomparable elixir of sunny Portugal as we
watched the dying embers of the fire turn to glowing ash. And so to
bed, for there is always another day tomorrow.

My walk this morning took me, by a zig-zag route, up the hillside
to the Upper Levels highway, an uphill climb of some four hundred
feet in a mile and a half of walking. As I climbed, the fog blanket
became noticeably less dense, and more detail became visible in my
immediate surroundings. The great and stately trees of our coast
forest, Douglas Fir, Western Hemlock, and Red Cedar are, in my

view, never more beautiful than when seen through a veil of mist or fog. Their characteristic shapes, in all their loveliness, are revealed in silhouette with distracting detail somewhat obscured, and the receding planes of distance become well separated, giving a rare sense of depth to the whole scene, a small symphony in gray tones. I must try to catch this effect in oil paint, some day soon. Paynes Gray, lightened with Titanium White, and the merest touch of Cerulean Blue, with increasing amounts of the white as the more distant planes are painted in; that should do it.

As I reached the quiet street that runs parallel to the Upper Levels highway, I suddenly emerged through the ceiling of the fog bank, and the morning sun, low in the heavens, came blazing out of a clear blue sky. The air had a pure, invigorating quality and all nature seemed to possess a clean, newly-washed appearance. On the far side of the highway, the mountain side rises steep and forest-clad above the granite rock cut flanking the road. A famous naturalist once said, "Forests are Nature's sanctuaries of pure water," and these forested mountains of Vancouver's North Shore are a testament to this assertion, for the whole area has been dedicated as a water district, secure from commercial, industrial, or other intrusion, whose ground water flows unpolluted into the reservoir behind the great Cleveland Dam, from which the city's fine water supply is obtained.

Here and there among the sombre stands of Douglas Fir, especially at the lower levels on the mountain side, one sees spinneys of the Red Alder, whose bare twigs, purplish-gray, and myriads of shiny winter catkins give the appearance of puffs of grayish smoke. In a few weeks, and after the inevitable onset of warmer days, the catkins will swell and change colour, and the still leafless alders will take on a most delicate purple tint, beautiful to behold, and one of the earliest harbingers of approaching spring.

The Red Alder is, in my opinion, a sadly under-appreciated tree in this area, where the word "tree" usually connotes the economically important giant conifers which are so characteristic of the Pacific Northwest. Broad-leaved, deciduous trees are in the minority here, and some, including the Red Alder, are regarded by many as weed trees, to be ruthlessly cleared away to make room for any "development" project, however trivial. But, unlike the small bush-like Alders that line the borders of lakes and streams in Eastern Canada, the western Red Alder can, and frequently does, attain a splendid size, with a noble straight trunk two feet or more in diameter, supporting a finely-shaped crown of spreading branches

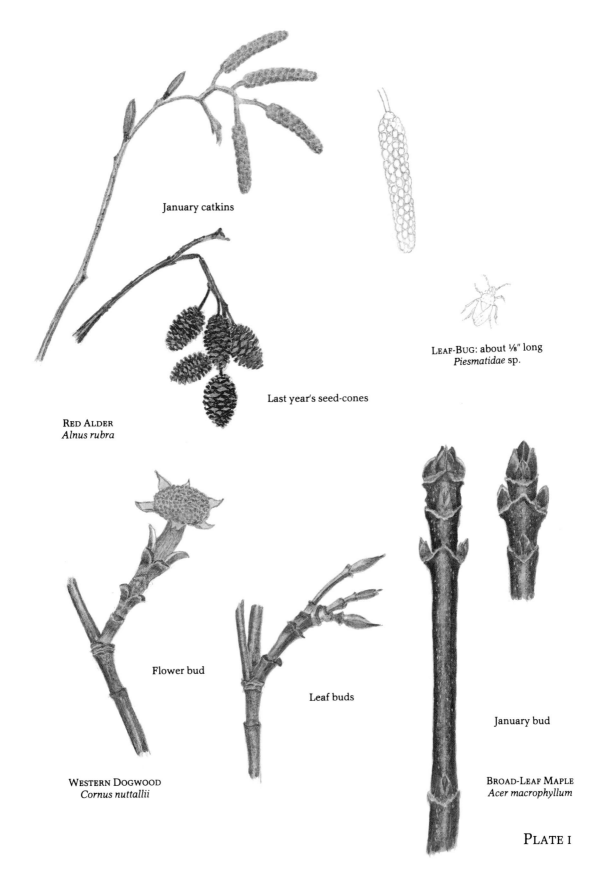

January catkins

LEAF-BUG: about ⅛″ long
Piesmatidae sp.

Last year's seed-cones

RED ALDER
Alnus rubra

Flower bud

Leaf buds

January bud

WESTERN DOGWOOD
Cornus nuttallii

BROAD-LEAF MAPLE
Acer macrophyllum

PLATE I

and clean ovate leaves. Moreover, the sawn trunks provide a most excellent firewood which, though not quite as high in caloric value as the celebrated hard maple and yellow birch of Eastern Canada, nevertheless burns cleanly and evenly, and with a fragrance surpassing that of any other firewood with which I am familiar.

But this morning, as I pursued my pedestrian way westward parallel to the Upper Level, and thence by another zig-zag route down through the fog towards my morning coffee, the Alders were in their deepest winter stage, the catkins – clusters of male flower buds – were hard, shiny and small, and interspersed here and there with bunches of the brown-black empty seed-cones of last year's female flowers, graceful and elegant still, though their work is long since done.

I brought home a few twigs of the Alder, in order to make a drawing, and while I was examining these, a very small insect, a hemipterous leaf-bug, appeared on the clean surface of my drawing board, having apparently fallen out of one of the empty seed cones I was holding in my hand (*Plate 1*). The early stages of this group of insects – the true "bugs" – are not too well understood, and I was mystified as to what an apparently mature leaf-bug was doing, alive and active, hiding in a seed cone in the very nadir of winter.

January 6 "Little Christmas," the Feast of the Epiphany. The Greek word, ἐπιφανης, means, approximately, "shining forth," but this is a darkling morning. The sea fog, which lasted several days, is now dispersed, but the sky is cloud-covered and lowering, with a suggestion of rain to come, though there is a promise of clearing later in the day. Although the winter solstice is more than two weeks past, the brightening of the morning is so far scarcely apparent. Due to certain complexities in the motion of the earth in its orbit, the sunrise continues to occur *later* in the morning for several days after the actual winter solstice. The sunset also occurs later each afternoon, and that by a somewhat greater daily difference, so that the actual hours and minutes of daylight are in fact increasing, but it is always well on into January before this becomes noticeable in the mornings.

This morning, I went down to the beach, and made my way for some distance along the shore. The tide was almost at the full, and I had to pick my way among the great logs of driftwood which are always present along the high-water line. As I appeared, a Great Blue Heron rose from his fishing with slow lazy wing-beats, arranged his spindly landing gear in the horizontal position, trailing behind him, arched his long neck back over his shoulders, and flapped noiselessly away to an undisturbed fishing spot further along the shore. A handsome pair of Red Breasted Mergansers came paddling energetically along, a few feet out from the waterline, dipping busily for food, and paying no attention to me or to anything else but the business in hand (*Plate 2*). Further out, a large group of Surf Scoters, possibly our commonest winter duck, seemed to be holding a well-mannered conference. Every few minutes, one of them, for some reason doubtless valid to a duck brain, but obscure to my limited human intelligence, would rise with a great whirring of wings, usually followed by a number of his fellows, only to settle down again at some presumably more attractive spot fifty or a hundred feet away. Someone has suggested to me that these are a select group, going off to discuss in detail some point of concern to surf scoters, with the intention of returning and making their report to the main body of ducks, in the approved manner of the modern "workshop" type conference.

The whirring of wings which accompanies this manoeuvre rises to a loud, shrill whistle, audible for a long distance over the surface of the sea. This appears to be common to most, if not all, duck species, but is particularly noticeable in the case of the scoters. It seems that ducks are relatively heavy-bodied birds, with somewhat short wings, so that the rapid wing beats that lead to the noisy whirring sound are necessary to their flight, and especially during "take-off" from the surface of the water. In contrast, our large and ever-present glaucous-winged gulls, with their wide span of narrow wings, are completely noiseless in flight, soaring, wheeling, using every air-current in their ceaseless and lovely aerial ballet.

The broad beach of barnacle-encrusted stones is now covered by the tide, and the barnacles, strange little crustaceans, each in its small stony fortress, will now have opened their trap doors and the marvellously modified legs will be rhythmically waving, to gather in the microscopic plankton on which the animal feeds. In six hours, the beach will again have become exposed by the receding tide, and every barnacle will have withdrawn its bunch of plume-like legs and tightly closed its trap door until the next flood tide brings another wealth of the life-giving treasure of the sea.

Some distance along the shore is a place where I habitually leave the beach to climb a narrow stone stairway through a spinney of woodland, taking me back to Marine Drive. Against the rich backdrop of forest evergreens, the now leafless deciduous trees seem bare and lifeless. But a closer look shows every twig laden

FEMALE

MALE

RED-BREASTED MERGANSERS
Mergus serrator

GREAT BLUE HERON
Ardea herodias

PLATE II

with buds full of burgeoning life eager to emerge. The Broad-leaf Maples, particularly, have very sturdy, masculine-looking buds, madder-brown in hue, geometrically placed in pairs opposite each other on the stem, each pair placed at right-angles to the pair above it and below it on the stem, in a very regular order. Such an arrangement naturally helps to determine the shape of the mature tree, with its beautiful dense crown. The Broad-leaf Maple is our only really large maple here on the coast. It does suffer, in the minds of some, by comparison with the magnificent hard maples of the east, with their spectacular autumn display of flaming red. But the Broad-leaf, with its great palmate leaves a rich golden yellow in the fall, is by no means lacking in autumn splendours of its own.

The winter buds of the Western Dogwood give immediate promise of the showy spectacle which will appear in May. Each bud, a small, round cushion of minute flower buds, green with a purplish tinge, stands on an elaborate-looking flower stalk, and is surrounded by six tiny leaflets which, in the fullness of time, will develop into the broad white "petals" – actually leaf bracts – that give the plant its well-merited reputation as British Columbia's official flower. The leaf buds occur in small groups on stalks separate from the flower buds, and in January appear as small spear heads of purplish-brown.

The unusually mild, moist weather is everywhere apparent. Today I *January 15* brought home a few sprigs of pussy willow as I usually do when they first appear as silvery downy buds bursting from shiny brown calyxes (*Plate 3*). This usually occurs in mid-February, and the sprigs of pussy willow look well in a tall vase with half-a-dozen of the earliest daffodils. But now, in mid-January, with the daffodils only just appearing as small, tentative green spikes, the pussy willows are already well advanced, and, placed in a vase this morning, they are already throwing out their halo of yellow stamens, and in a couple of days, influenced by the indoor warmth, will be shedding their layer of pollen on the oak table-top where they stand.

Willows must surely be the most ubiquitous, as well as the most confusing, botanically, of all the trees of the temperate zone. Running into hundreds of species, they flourish in all kinds of habitat, and occur in all shapes and sizes, from the magnificent trees that bend their branches over streams, and inhabit flat lands all over the more southerly areas of North America, Europe and Asia, to the tiny, low-growing but unbelievably hardy species that flourish in the northern perma-frost, right up to the edge of the "high Arctic." Confronted with a specimen of willow catkin, it is very difficult to say with certainty what exact species it is. Therefore, in assigning a caption to my sketch of the pussy willow, I take refuge in the taxonomist's standard method of confessing ignorance, and call it *Salix sp.* – "a species of" Willow.

Today as I climb the stiff slope adjacent to McKechnie Park, two ravens appear, soaring above the big hemlock trees that rise thickly in this fine little stand of virgin timber. There seems always to be a small population of ravens here, and I am often greeted as I pass with their hoarse, deep, croaking call, so different from the sharp bark of the ever-present carrion crows which, except for the larger size, the ravens so closely resemble. The crows seem to have been growing increasingly numerous over the past few years. Their cheerful, noisy clamour from the treetops is the commonest early-morning sound. They are useful scavengers, and do well on the bits of carrion and edible debris always present along the sea shore. They also vie with the neighbourhood dogs in making havoc of the garbage set out by the local citizens on garbage day, in readiness for the weekly visit of the municipal trash collectors.

The crows are also a great nuisance, later in the year, to the robins, whose nests they rob of eggs and hatchlings in the early days of spring. But the robins show a surprising talent for concerted action when one of their nests is threatened. At the first strident note of alarm from an indignant parent bird, there appear, almost in a twinkling, six, ten, a dozen, a score of infuriated robins, harrying and dive-bombing the marauding crow and sometimes, though not always, diverting it from its fell purpose.

The bird books tell us that there are three distinct species of crow that find this seashore habitat hospitable to them, the "common" or broad-billed crow (*brachyrhyncus*), the north-western crow (*caurinus*) and the fish-crow (*ossifragus*), all members of the genus *Corvus* – the Crow. They are said to differ slightly in size and some other minor characteristics, but I am not enough of an ornithologist to tell them apart, and I content myself with thinking of them as "crows." But I do not confuse them with the "common" Raven (*Corvus corax*), whose much larger size, and elderly senatorial voice are, as the textbooks say, "diagnostic."

During these January days, the roadside ditches are untidy with the dead remains of last summer's flowering plants, now sere and brown. Many of these, though untidy and unkempt in the mass, are individually graceful and elegant. There is a current fad for collecting these seeded flower heads, staining them in bright colours and using them in bouquets for house decoration. I prefer the muted browns, yellows and silver-grays of the unimproved article. To quote Shakespeare's *King John*:

> To gild refined gold, to paint the lily,
> To throw a perfume on the violet,
> Were wanton and ridiculous excess.

A very large proportion of the common flowering plants that brighten our roadsides during spring and summer are not indigenous to this area at all, but are invaders from Europe and Asia. When the continent was first colonized, the pioneers brought their animals with them, on shipboard, together with the necessary bales of hay for feed, until sources from the cleared land could be depended upon. The seeds of many of the common wayside weeds of the Old World were the most natural and obvious of stowaways in the bales of hay, and most seem to have found the new habitat to their liking. One of the more conspicuous of these landed immigrants of the plant world, which brightens our local roadsides in late summer and fall, is the St. John's Wort (or "Sinjun-wort" as it is called by some English people who seem to feel that familiarity with, and use of, such absurd mispronunciations affords them some kind of social distinction). But this very hardy plant, with its dense heads of golden yellow, star-shaped flowers (*Plate 4*), is said to have received its name from an ancient superstition that it possessed certain curative qualities which were operative only on June 24th, the Festal Day of Saint John. The Baptist, not the Evangelist .

Culpeper's Compleat Herbal, that quaint 17th century compendium of folk remedies, does not overtly attribute the healing qualities of St. John's Wort to the beatific influence of the good Saint, but Nicholas Culpeper, an astrologer as well as a physician, has this to say about the hardy weed:

> It is under the celestial sign of Leo. . . St. John's Wort is aperative, detersive, and diuretic, helpful against tertian and quartan agues, is alexipharmic, and destroys worms. . .
> . . . The decoction of the herb and flowers, especially the seed, being drunk in wine with the juice of knot-grass, helps all manner of spitting of blood, and vomiting; it is good also for those who cannot make water and are bitten by venomous creatures.
> . . . The seed, taken in warm wine, is recommended for sciatica, falling-sickness, and the palsy. It is vulnerary, abstersive, opens obstructions, and scours the urinary passages.

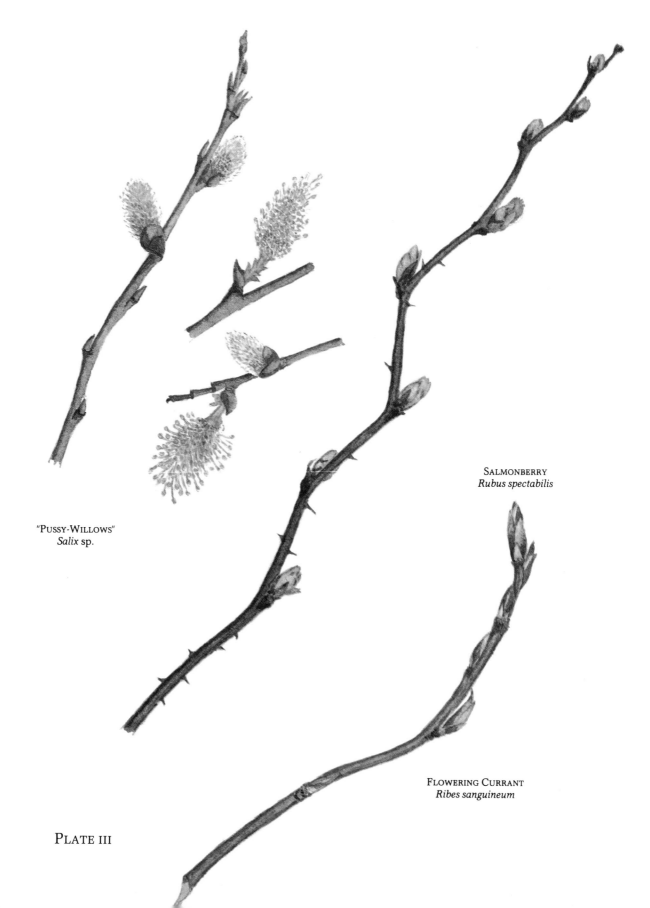

"PUSSY-WILLOWS"
Salix sp.

SALMONBERRY
Rubus spectabilis

FLOWERING CURRANT
Ribes sanguineum

PLATE III

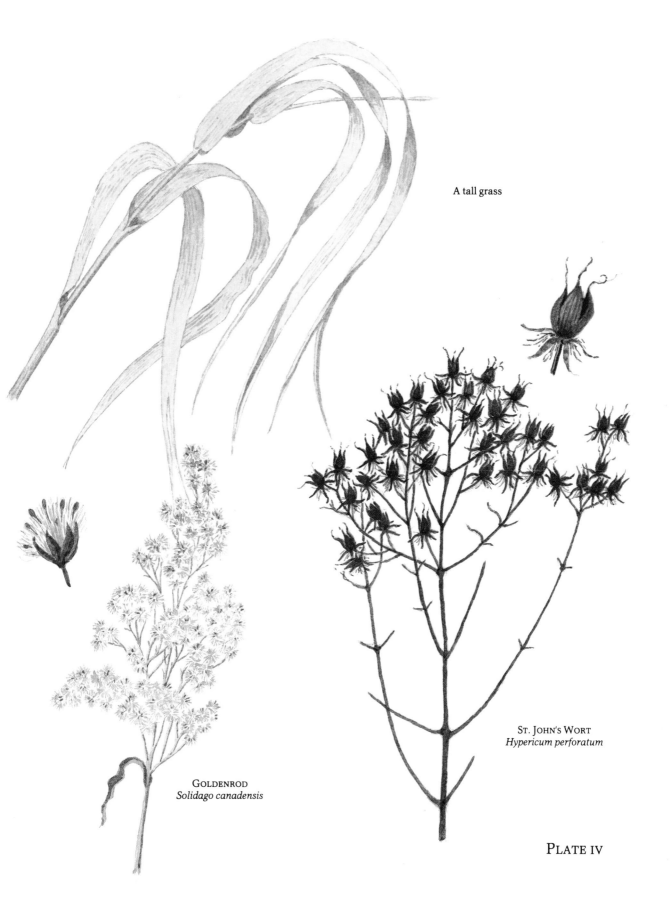

A tall grass

GOLDENROD
Solidago canadensis

St. John's Wort
Hypericum perforatum

PLATE IV

Good. I must try it some time. Some other time. I wonder why it is that, down the centuries, the reputations of the undoubtedly valuable medicinal properties of a great many common herbs have been diluted by so much unmitigated balderdash!

But here on January 15, 1981, the plants are dead wraiths of their former selves, the yellow flowers replaced by a wealth of small brown-black empty seed capsules.

January 20 This morning I am walking in the rain, a gentle rain falling from a bright sky, and I am enjoying it. I do not make a fetish of walking resolutely in every kind of weather, rain or shine. I do not enjoy getting drenched, neither do I like sweltering in a cocoon of heavy rubberized raingear. But a little rain, within reason, never hurt anyone, and, indeed, "rain-in-the-face and wind-in-the-hair" can be quite pleasant and invigorating sensations.

As I stride along, engrossed in my thoughts, I narrowly miss treading on a handsome black slug. His barely visible contrail of silvery mucus reveals that he has crossed the twenty-two foot roadway from the woods of McKechnie Park, and is now within a foot of the ditch at the opposite side of the road. At the rate at which he travels, this must be a journey of at least an hour and a half. That he has survived thus far without being flattened by a passing automobile, even on this relatively lightly travelled route, seems to me one of nature's small miracles. In order not to tempt Providence further than necessary, after a brief examination I transport him, with a quick flip of my walking stick, at jet-age speed over the remaining foot or so of his journey into the presumably greener pastures he was making for, where he can recover at leisure from his astonishment, if indeed slugs possess a mentality capable of astonishment, which I am inclined to doubt.

These strange shell-less land-molluscs, or gastropods, are anathema to our local gardeners in this area, for they often appear in large numbers and inflict serious depredations on tender garden seedlings. The somewhat larger spotted slug (*Limax maximus*), rather startling coloured in mustard-yellow with dark brown spots, does not seem to be common in this particular locality. This black fellow (*Arion ster*), is the one we usually see (*Plate 5*).

The Salal bushes, as well as the great trumpet-like Sword-ferns look especially fresh and glossy in the rain. The Salal, a member of the enormous Heather family (*Ericaceae*) is without question the predominant plant constituting the ground cover, or underbrush, of the coastal rain forest. It is not only the great forest conifers themselves that have earned for this North Pacific coast the reputation of "evergreen paradise," but quite equally the preponderance of broad-leaved evergreen trees and shrubs of which the Salal is a typical example. Its tough, woody stems and dense cover of thick, strong leaves often make foot travel in the coastal bush very difficult indeed, an underbrush as dense and as worthy of the term "impenetrable" as anything I have encountered in the tropical mountain forest of the Venezuelan Andes.

But the Salal plant itself is a handsome one, with clusters of beautiful shell-pink bell-shaped flowers to appear later in the year, and blue-black berries in the fall, from which the native people concoct a medicinal brew. There is, also, a considerable commerce in Salal greenery with the florists of Eastern Canada, who use it for embellishment of their "floral tributes."

At one of the three places where I habitually pause for a few moments on my uphill walk, the roadside rock on which I sit is backed by a dense low thicket of Salal and Sword-fern, which affords excellent cover for a mini-population of small winter birds; the Towhee, with its mournful winter call from which its name is derived, the Oregon Junco, the Chickadee and the Winter Wren. There is usually a small murmur of twittering conversation going on in there behind me as I sit, and a furtive, and mostly unseen coming and going of feathered bodies.

The Sword-ferns seem eternal, and are at their greenest just now. Later in the spring, the graceful "fiddle-heads" of the new fronds will appear as a small group in the middle of the plant, and as the old outer fronds wither and die, the new ones will develop from the furry fiddle-heads to perpetuate the evergreen appearance of this graceful plant, my favourite among the many species of fern that inhabit the area.

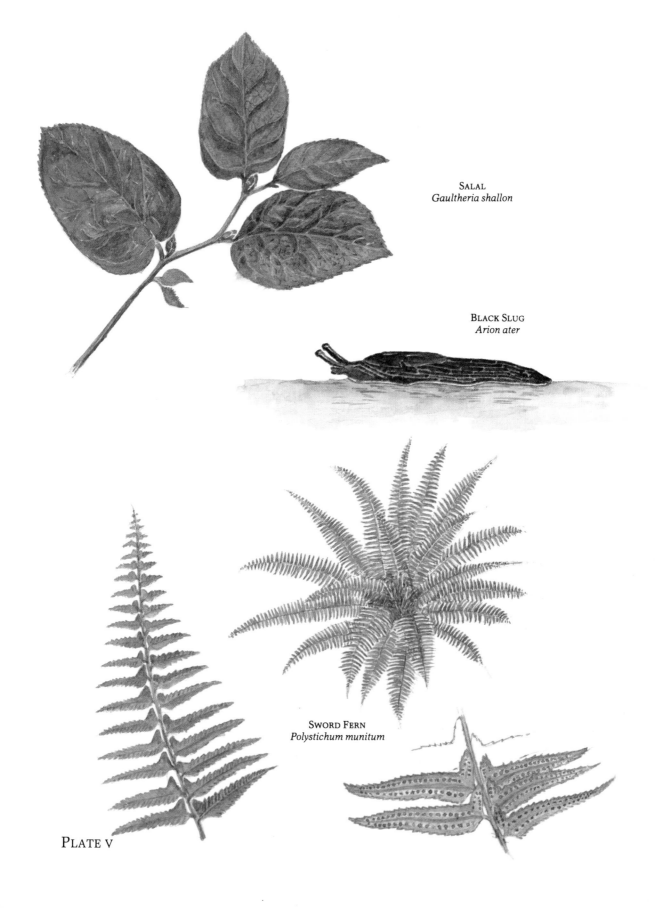

SALAL
Gaultheria shallon

BLACK SLUG
Arion ater

SWORD FERN
Polystichum munitum

PLATE V

February

Candle-mass, according to the church calendar; Ground-hog Day to more secular minds. As I set out this morning, a bright but overcast and quite pleasant day, it was evident the ground-hog was not seeing his shadow, at least not at the moment. But there seems a promise of clear sunshine to come later in the day, and history does not relate at what hour of the day the ground-hog's prognostications are to be taken as valid. I wonder where these old sayings originate, and on what they are based? In my early childhood in the south of England, I had never heard of a ground-hog, but it was the Bear who, emerging from hibernation, forecast the weather for the next forty days, according to whether he saw, or did not see, his shadow cast by the early spring sun. In Germany it was neither bear nor ground-hog, but the Badger. *Der Dachs auf Lichtmess* – "The Badger at Candlemass" – was one of my required-reading texts when learning German at high school during the First World War. But here in West Vancouver, the bear would seem to be more appropriate than either badger or ground-hog, for the badger is a rare animal, and ground-hogs we do not commonly see. For the ground-hog, or "wood-chuck" (or more properly, "American Marmot"), is a creature of the open fields, a familiar nuisance to farmers in the eastern part of the continent. Two related species we do have, the Yellow-bellied and the Hoary Marmots, but these keep to the high mountain meadows and are not seen here along the coast.

But the Black Bear is a not uncommon denizen of our nearby wooded mountain slopes. Its visits to these areas where I walk are less frequent since the Upper Levels highway has been completed, for wild animals do not willingly cross such a traffic-ridden barrier which, to ursine nostrils, no doubt reeks of Man and his works. However, the highway does traverse, by means of high bridges, the ravines and canyons of the many mountain streams, and large animals find their way down these ravines from time to time, undeterred by the sound of traffic far above their heads. So that occasionally a local resident, peering wan-eyed from a bedroom window in the early morning, will be startled by the sight of a she-bear and cubs investigating the contents of the garbage can, to the great excitement of the children, the alarm of their mothers, and the considerable worry of the local police and wildlife people. Rendered incautious by cuddly nursery tales of friendly bears, children – of all ages – are apt to become far too confident in the presence of what are, in fact, powerful, unpredictable, and potentially dangerous animals. There is a new, and very commendable reluctance to destroying these innocent wild creatures, but their capture and removal to a more acceptable area is a difficult, costly and time-consuming operation.

February 16   After a night of heavy rain, the sun rose this morning into a clear sky. The temperature is at a mild 11° Celsius, and there is a distinct sniff of spring in the air. I walked again along the beach. The sea was at half-tide, and, for most of the way the broad space of hard-packed sand between the waterline and the inevitable bastion of piled driftwood made for pleasant easy walking. The little streams that find their way down the mountainside, swollen by the nocturnal downpour, had become roaring torrents, and our nearby Cypress Creek, for the next few hours, is a raging river. Where it crosses the beach and pours itself into the bay, a large congregation of seagulls and crows were gathered, eagerly availing themselves of the goodies brought down by the swollen creek.

But, as I stood watching them an intruder appeared – other than myself – a large adult white-tailed or "bald" eagle, soaring majestically against the blue (*Plate 6*). In very short order, it was set upon by a flight of noisy crows, for, just as the crows themselves are "mobbed" by outraged robins, these great eagles are commonly harried by crows, though, as far as one can see with far less reason. For the eagle, a predator principally upon fish, can surely pose little threat to the crow, a carrion feeder. But presumably anyone so much larger than oneself is automatically to be regarded as a foe, and should be driven off, if possible, by force of numbers.

This magnificent and peace-loving bird, now rare and on the endangered species list in the country which has adopted it as a national emblem, is actually a fairly common – though protected – denizen of this North Pacific coast. A pair frequently nests in the woods of nearby Lighthouse Park, always at the top of one of the tallest trees – preferably one with a bare "snag" top – where a full 360° viewpoint can be assured. They are a fairly common sight along our sea front, the mature birds, and sometimes the immature young, their white head and tail plumage not yet developed. But what, oh what unobservant observer it was that first dubbed them "bald," a

WHITE-TAILED OR "BALD" EAGLE
Haliaeetus leucocephalus

PLATE VI

term that calls to mind the featherless, wrinkled, and faintly revolting head and neck of the turkey-vulture—a wise dispensation of nature in the case of the turkey-vulture, which often feeds with its head and neck buried in a carrion carcass. But the American eagle, so far from being bald, carries a rich white mane that would do justice to an elderly senator, or a Supreme Court judge. The scientific nomenclature honours it more fittingly in the specific name *leucocephalus*—white-headed. But I can never become blase about a sighting of this noble bird, its seven-foot span of broad brown-black wings almost motionless as it rides the air currents, making "lazy circles in the sky," its snowy head and tail gleaming in the low morning sun. It thrills me always; the White-tailed Eagle it will always be. Bald-eagle, never!

February 28   The last day of February, and the first truly spring-like day of the year. The sun, shining out of a clear cerulean sky, is beginning to exhibit some power. On my walk up the hillside this morning, I found myself entering a sudden fairyland of flowering trees, transfiguring the gardens of the good West Vancouver citizens—the rose-pink of flowering plum, the shell-pink of the ornamental cherry, other trees a cloud of snowy white, the Forsythia bushes a blaze of golden yellow. At one point, a rose-pink Camellia bush, in a sheltered spot, is in full bloom, though our own Camellias, somewhat less favourably placed, are still exhibiting only fat buds. But we do have a pink Rhododendron and a white Azalea already in flower. I wish them luck, for we still have blustery March to face. But these coastal mountains are a natural habitat for Rhododendrons, and wild species of this acid-loving plant are still to be found in our woods. So even the more spectacular cultivated varieties are relatively hardy here.

We did honour to the delightfully warm day by taking luncheon *al fresco* on our patio, overlooking a sparkling blue bay, on which a multitude of sailboat enthusiasts are making the most of their Saturday freedom. As we sat, an Angle-wing butterfly, fresh out of hibernation, sailed over our heads, fluttered for a moment against the picture-window, and continued swiftly on its way. The first I have seen this spring, and it is always, for me, a small Special Event. These stout-bodied, rapid-flying Angle-wings always seem to be the first to be cajoled out of their winter hidey holes by the strengthening sun. They belong to a large genus of butterflies of the North Temperate Zone, which has been given the name *Polygonia*—many angles—in reference to the angular, almost jagged shape of the wings. Our early visitor is of the common local species *Polygonia satyrus*, and has the usual colour-scheme of the genus, tawny orange-brown, with spots and bars of glossy black. The underside of these powerful little pinions, however, is of dull unobtrusive gray, so that when the insect is at rest, with wings over back, and especially when in hibernation in some sheltered corner, the dull colouring together with the jagged outline of the closed wings produces an extraordinary resemblance to a withered leaf, or a bit of loose bark. A peculiarity of these butterflies is the tiny silver "hallmark" in the centre of this dull underside of the wings, the purpose of which is not understood. The shape of this mark varies somewhat in the different species of the genus. One species well-known to British naturalists has its mark in the shape of a comma, and is therefore called the "Comma butterfly." Another species, occurring in the eastern part of this continent carries a mark shaped like a point-of-interrogation, and is, appropriately enough, named by taxonomists *Polygonia interrogationis*, the "Question-sign butterfly." Our own little *P. satyrus* has a silver mark that resembles not much of anything at all except, perhaps, a minute Australian boomerang! Rather than push the imagination too far, we just call it the "Angle-wing butterfly."

The stands of alder, among the dark firs of the mountainside, have already taken on their distant appearance of purplish smoke, from the myriads of ripening catkins, which were so small, hard, and shiny in early January, but which now are long and pendulous, hanging in groups of three or four from the extremity of every twig. On some, the multitude of minute flowers have already opened, and discharged their cloud of almost impalpably fine yellow pollen (*Plate 7*).

RED ALDER
Alnus rubra
Mature catkins

AMERICAN ROBIN
Turdus migratorius

ANGLE-WING BUTTERFLY
Polygonia satyrus

EVENING GROSBEAK
(recovering)
Hesperiphona vespertina

PLATE VII

March

The old adage about March "coming in like a lion" does not seem to have materialized this year. These first few days of the Mad Month have been chiefly mild and pleasant, with occasional showers of gentle rain, interspersed with patches of robin's-egg sky, and great masses of billowy cumulus cloud piled high above Grouse Mountain and the Lions. But the green explosion of spring has begun, and even the slowest of the deciduous trees are showing the first "fuzz" of new leaves. On the Salmonberry bushes, the handsome five-petalled rose-pink flowers are already open, somewhat ahead of the leaves, which are just starting to unfurl and not yet arranged in their orderly formation of three leaflets to a stem.

Perhaps most remarkable for the rapidity of its spring growth is the common, or trailing blackberry, which appears to invade with great eagerness any area of these north shore slopes where the native forest growth has been cleared away. In mid-February, a brilliant green tuft of new leaves appeared at each point where the withered axils of the old leaves spring from the great sturdy stems. By now, these small tufts have grown into spreading rosettes of new leaves, largely enveloping the dull and fading greenery of last year (*Plate 8*). When I contemplate one of our well-developed blackberry thickets I am reminded of the storybook illustrations of the *Sleeping Beauty* which were so beautifully executed by the famous nineteenth-century illustrators, Arthur Rackham and Edmund Dulac. The great squarish stems, almost an inch in girth, with their wicked re-curved thorns, often seem more like something out of a fairy-tale than a common vegetable reality. At the height of growing season one can almost fancy one can actually see the blackberry runners increasing in length as one watches. From the unused property at the foot of my garden, a determined and irrepressible army of blackberry brambles has to be kept continuously at bay by the ceaseless application of sickle and shears. But in the summer these become a lovely blaze of white blossoms to delight the eye and attract a cloud of butterflies, and in August we are rewarded with a copious black harvest of the luscious fruit. But in order to win this harvest with a minimum of bloodshed, I find it necessary to dress somewhat like a mediaeval man-at-arms, for the merciless thorns claw at the intruder in the most determined manner, and the lacerations can be severe. Another, though nowadays less common hazard, when harvesting blackberries in the less frequented corners of our mountainside area, becomes apparent when one finds oneself peering through the thicket at the little pig eyes of a bear, equally intent on the ripe fruit. The black bear's love-affair with the blackberry is enshrined in the botanical name of the plant, *Rubus ursinus*.

March 24   I have just returned from a ten days' absence in Eastern Canada, during which it was necessary to take my daily walks in somewhat less familiar surroundings. Today, returning to my usual route up the mountainside, I find the spring already far advanced in many ways. But possibly the most noticeable difference is one of *sound*. For the birds are returning in force from the south and beginning to make their presence felt and heard. In this relatively mild climate, we have many species of birds, some of which are content to spend the winter with us. But during the winter months these birds are for the most part quite silent, their vocalizations consisting chiefly of quiet conversational twitterings among the bushes. But on this, my first day's walk after the brief absence, it is very noticeable that the numbers of birds are substantially increased. The travellers are returning, courtship has obviously started, male birds are busily staking out their territory and telling others about it in their own time-honoured and inimitable way. The sharp repetitive shout of the Flicker and the so-welcome territorial call of the Robin seem to ring out from all quarters.

> In the Spring, a fuller crimson
> Comes upon the robin's breast

Tennyson's robin was, of course, the European "robin redbreast," a smaller and rather different bird from our well-loved American Robin, which is really a species of Thrush — *Turdus migratorius* — whose breast is not crimson but russet-red. But the tame and confiding ways of "our" robin must have reminded the early settlers of those same endearing characteristics in their familiar robin-red-breast, and Robin it became and to us will always be. Very soon we shall be digging in the garden, and there will always be at least one robin within two or three feet of the garden-fork awaiting the inevitable disinterment of a luscious worm dinner.

Demands upon our bird-feeder are already noticeably increased. In addition to Towhees, Juncos and Chickadees which patronize us throughout the winter, other recently-arrived species are now coming after the grain and sunflower seeds – House Finches with their pretty red polls, Evening Grosbeaks, and of course that inevitable arch-comedian of the feathered world, the Steller's Jay, with his gorgeous blue and black plumage and his impudent beady black eye – not to mention his insatiable, greedy appetite.

I was distressed, this morning, on returning home from my *March 30* customary three miles, to find on the ground under our front window, the dead body of a robin, still warm, its neck broken, and on the window above a small telltale tuft of adhering poll feathers. The modern vogue for large "picture" or "view" windows, with big undivided panes of glass, takes a heavy toll of small birds, especially during the spring and fall migrations. These windows, kept highly polished by house-proud owners, display a bright reflected image of the sky and treetops in front of them which is highly confusing to a flying bird. It is true that some birds, robins for instance, during the frenzy of nesting and territory-claiming, will often attack their own reflected image in such a window, but this is merely comical to a human observer and seldom, if ever, results in injury to anyone. But a migrating bird, flying full-throttle into what it takes to be a continuation of treetops and open sky, and smashing into a rock-hard, invisible, and totally unsuspected sheet of window-glass, is a different matter altogether. At such a speed, even the very small mass of a flying bird produces a terrific impact, which more often than not proves fatal from a broken neck. Sometimes, however, if the neck is not actually broken, and the little creature still shows signs of life, it is possible to revive it in the warmth of the cupped hands, and the powers of recovery are sometimes truly remarkable. I have often brought in to the house such an injured mite, and nursed it back to health simply by warmth. On one or two occasions I have administered a few drops of whiskey and water, by means of an eye-dropper, to help the restorative process. My ornithological friends do not applaud this treatment, but at times, I have found its effect to be salutary!

On one such occasion, I brought in a stunned Evening Grosbeak, which still showed signs of life, and nursed it in my two hands until it began to fidget. Then, sitting cross-legged in my favourite arm chair, I placed the little bird, right-side up, on my left knee, where it stayed for twenty minutes while I drew its portrait, catching its

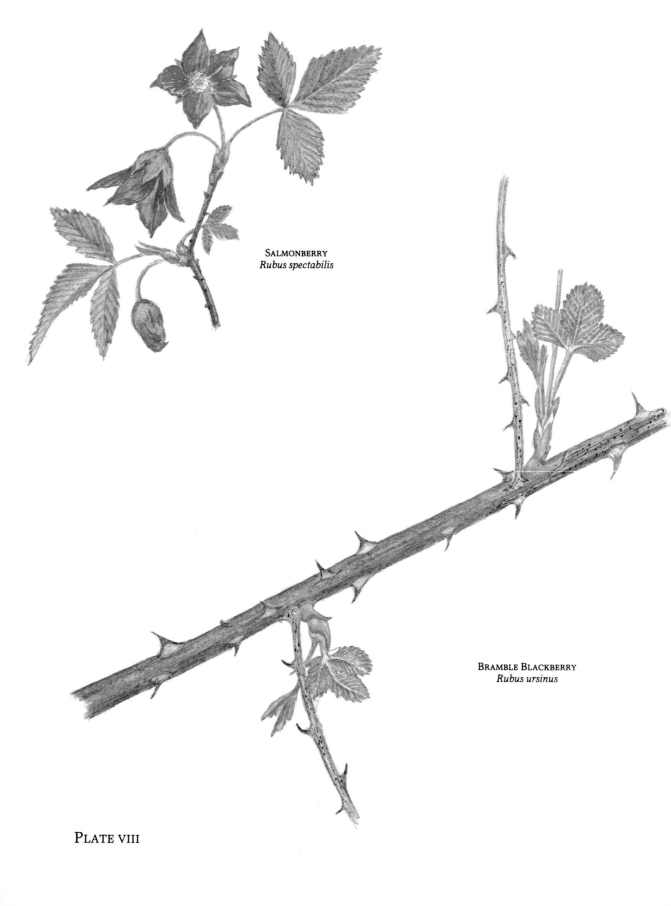

SALMONBERRY
Rubus spectabilis

BRAMBLE BLACKBERRY
Rubus ursinus

PLATE VIII

beautiful colours, as far as I was able, with coloured pencils, while it sat perfectly still wearing a comical expression of confused puzzlement, as though attempting to recall the events leading up to the accident. Eventually, and without any vocal warning, it flew up onto the valance-board above the window, and I had the greatest difficulty in catching it again and putting it outside to resume its rudely interrupted journey.

But today's victim was well beyond recall, and after briefly stretching out one of its wings to wonder again at its beauty, I took a spade and buried the little corpse, lest it should be defiled by a marauding cat. I love cats, but am repelled by some of their carnivorous habits. Pure sentimentality, I suppose, for the buried bird would equally and immediately be seized upon by beetles and their grubs, ants, worms, and other such small underground denizens, simply carrying out the functions which nature intended for them.

April

April 1   I have managed to survive the morning of All Fools' Day without falling victim to any of the small practical jokes which my Constant Companion likes to subject me to on this particular date each year. And, setting forth on my morning walk, I find nature too in a benign mood, for it is sunny and reasonably mild for the time of year. In the ditch across the road from where, for a few moments, I sat on a rocky outcrop to catch my breath on the uphill climb, there is a small bush of Flowering Currant now in full bloom. In January I took home a twig of this common plant, in order to draw the winter buds. Today the bush is a glory of blood-red blossoms, so well justifying its botanical name, *Ribes sanguineum*. So I have now brought home with me another spray of this beautiful plant, and am about to start a drawing of it in its present and most lovely stage (*Plate 9*).

There is, close to the roadside flanking McKechnie Park, a small area cleared of underbrush, where early each spring a variety of native wild plants make their appearance. I noticed, this morning, that several heads of the large Horse-Tail, or Mare's-Tail plant have pushed themselves through the surface of the ground, and are now displaying their strange shapes six or eight inches above the surrounding cover. The Horse-Tail, with its odd segmented stem, is apparently a very primitive plant form, for fossil plants are frequently found in coal deposits, from which our present-day Horse-tail is almost indistinguishable in physical form. My late father, a truly Christian gentleman, but a Victorian, inclined to be somewhat Fundamentalist in his theological beliefs, used to say of the Horse-Tail that it was "a plant which survived the Flood." Be that as it may, it is strange that, whereas the vast majority of natural species, when compared with their fossil ancestors, display in the clearest manner the slow mutation and changes that have resulted from long aeons in the continuing process of Creation, yet there are, here and there, a few species of plant and animal which, like the common Horse-Tail, appear to have defied the winds of change and remained more or less unchanged from their original form. In a very short time, our Horse-Tails will throw out, from each segment of the stem, a whorl of graceful, bright-green, hair-shaped leaves, which are said to have given the plant its common name. I personally see, in this odd plant, little resemblance to Dobbin's caudal appendage, but the reference to a horse seems to have been perpetuated in the name of the genus, *Equisetum*.

The Horse-Tail, in full leaf, is a plant of delicate beauty, but it can be a great nuisance in the garden. Propagating itself from underground root-runners as well as from its own seed-spores, once it becomes established in a flower-bed, it is virtually impossible to eradicate except by deep-digging over a wide area. When we bought our West Vancouver property early in 1963 and started work on the garden, our good neighbour, Jean Pylot spoke darkly of something she referred to as "municipal weed." Enquiry among my botanist friends shed no light on this strange nomenclature, but Horse-Tail began to appear among our azaleas in quantities we little approved of. When we came to know our charming neighbours a little better, it transpired that, when Jean and Steve first acquired and built on their property, next to ours, there was no Horse-Tail; but subsequently, the municipality of West Vancouver deposited, in the public lane between our lots, a load of "fill," evidently obtained from an area where Horse-Tail was rife. The Pylots, and subsequently we ourselves, have struggled to control "municipal weed" ever since!

The true spring butterflies are starting to make their appearance. Those like the Angle-wing and the Milbert Tortoise-shell, which have awakened out of hibernation are still to be seen on warm days, sunning their outstretched wings on a rock, or rising unexpectedly from the roadside, unseen until I am almost upon them. Although somewhat faded, and often a little tattered from their long winter wait, they seem as bright as gems in the strengthening sun.

April 7

But the "true" spring butterflies are those which have over-wintered as chrysalids and are now newly emerged as mature insects. Invariably, the first of these to become noticeable is the so-called "Cabbage-white" – a scourge to vegetable-growers – but this morning I was delighted to see, also, flitting among the low herbage, one of the delicate little "Orange-tip" butterflies, the bright orange apical patch on the otherwise white wings shining in the sun, until the insect settled and closed its wings over its back, then revealing only the green-and-white chequered underside and rendering it very difficult to see among the spring leaves.

The "Cabbage-white" is not really a native insect, but in 120 years it has become a well-established colonist. The late W.J. Holland,

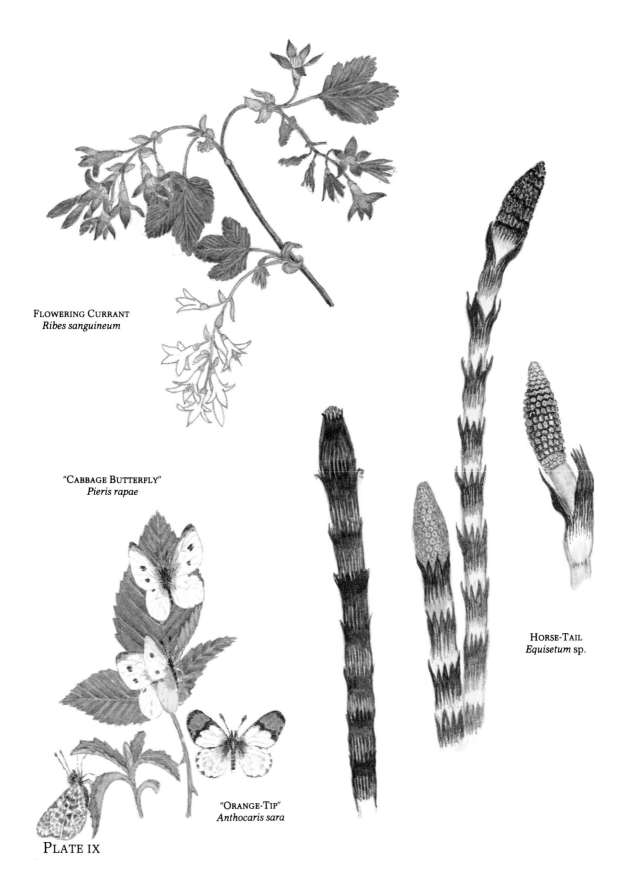

FLOWERING CURRANT
Ribes sanguineum

"CABBAGE BUTTERFLY"
Pieris rapae

HORSE-TAIL
Equisetum sp.

"ORANGE-TIP"
Anthocaris sara

PLATE IX

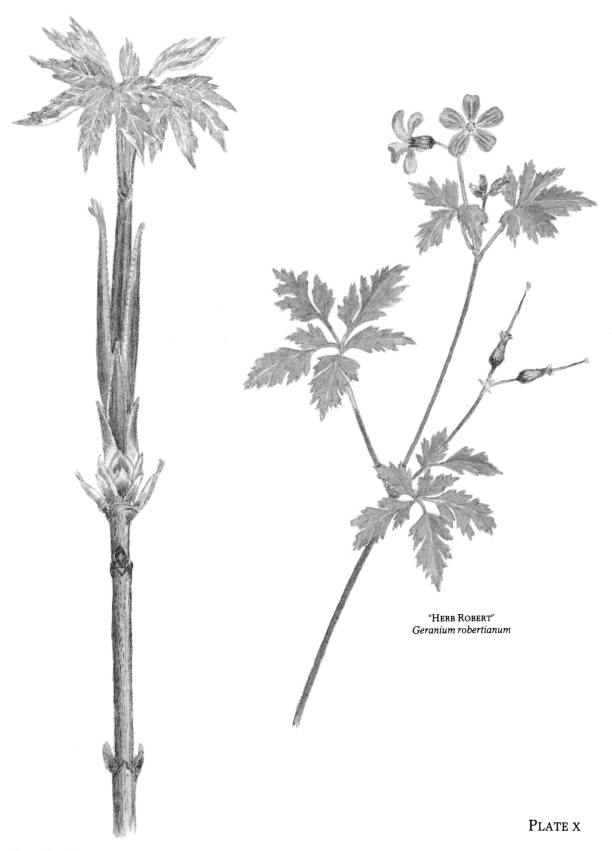

"HERB ROBERT"
Geranium robertianum

PLATE X

BROAD-LEAF MAPLE
Acer macrophyllum

author of the famous (but now out-of-print) *Butterfly Book* writing in 1898, had this to say about it:

> The insect reached Quebec about 1860. How it came, no man knows; perhaps in a load of cabbages from abroad; maybe a fertile female was brought over as a stowaway. At all events, it came. Estimates show that a single female might, in a few generations, be the progenitor of millions. In 1863 the butterfly was already common about Quebec, and was spreading rapidly. By 1881 it had spread over the entire eastern half of the continent, the advancing line of colonization reaching from Hudson's Bay to southern Texas. In 1886 it reached Denver, as in 1884 it had reached the headwaters of the Missouri, and it now (in 1898) possesses the cabbage-fields from the Atlantic to the Pacific, to the incalculable damage of all who provide the raw material for sauerkraut!

As Dr. Holland was himself a member of a naturalized East-European family, it is perhaps natural that this last-named aspect of the situation should be important to him! Yet this vigorously-thriving insect is actually not the "true" Cabbage-butterfly. That distinction belongs properly to a related, similarly marked, but much larger species from the Old World, appropriately named *Pieris brassicae* (from the Latin *brassica* – cabbage) which, however, has not found its way to this continent. But the voracious habits of the smaller colonist are well-expressed in its scientific name, *Pieris rapae*!

April 13   Although the changes in the appearance of my surroundings during my daily passings-by are not easy to detect from day to day, yet the whole aspect of the roadside is radically altered over the past two or three weeks. The sere and dry relics of last year's plants are now lost in a soft ground-cover of greenery. Small wild plants have appeared, as if by magic and added their spread leaves to the general carpet. Very apparent along the roadside ditches is the little wild geranium or "Crane's Bill," bearing the common name of "Herb Robert" (*Plate 10*). The origin of this Old World name is obscure; some say it has reference to the famous aristocratic outlaw Robin Hood, but in what connection, I have no idea. In any event, the name "Robin" has been preserved in the plant's botanical name, *Geranium robertianum*. The attractive rose-pink flowers, dotted like small pink stars among a wealth of beautiful finely-divided leaves, are familiar to everyone,

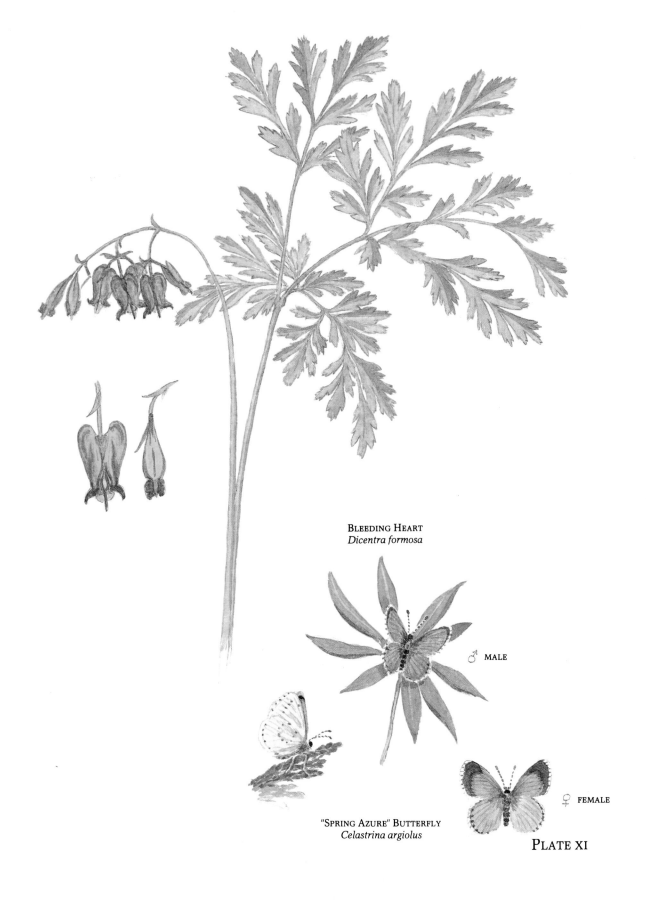

BLEEDING HEART
Dicentra formosa

♂ MALE

♀ FEMALE

"SPRING AZURE" BUTTERFLY
Celastrina argiolus

PLATE XI

for the plant invades gardens and roadside patches everywhere, with its stout hairy red stems and its strong, rank odour.

Here and there the tall nodding stems of the common Bleeding-Heart rise above the surrounding masses of grass and Herb Robert, with broad sprays of somewhat similarly shaped, finely-divided leaves and hanging rows of the strange more-or-less heart-shaped flowers, which call to my mind with a touch of nostalgia, two other members of the same Dicentra genus, the Squirrel-corn and the Dutchman's Breeches, both so familiar to me during my years in Eastern Canada (*Plate 11*).

Also just starting to display its small five-petalled yellow blossoms is the common Yellow Avens, or Geum, somewhat surprisingly a member of the Rose family (*Plate 12*). The surprise is, perhaps, only due to the somewhat insignificant flowers, only one or two at a time of which appear on each plant, surmounting a tall stem arising from a rosette of very large, handsome three-lobed leaves. In fact, the plant bears the specific name *macrophyllum* in honour of those big leaves. But one feels, somehow, that anything related to a rose ought to manage something in the way of a flower a bit more impressive than this poor little yellow star! A very unscientific thought, no doubt, of which I ought to be thoroughly ashamed!

April 19   Easter Day, and a morning full of sunshine, warmth and joy, such as Easter ought to be. The waters of the bay are blue and gleaming, and already dotted with white sails from the nearby yacht clubs.

This morning I saw the first blue butterfly, our common "Spring Azure" so-called, which is always a harbinger of approaching summer. This one was a female, with her tiny blue wings bearing a darker area on the forward wing-tips, or "apical angles." The males are of a brighter blue, and do not bear the darker markings. But the species is a puzzling one; the butterfly produces more than one brood during the year, and there are slight differences between the broods which have, in the past, caused confusion among lepidopterists, not only here, but also in Britain where the same insect occurs and is popularly known as the "Holly Blue," from the circumstance that its caterpillar feeds on the prickly Christmas shrub. Strangely, although the Holly has long ago been introduced into western North America, and flourishes mightily in this area, the spring Azure caterpillars do not seem to have taken it on as a food-plant, but stick to their ancestral North American diet of the Flowering Dogwood, our much-prized provincial flower. Yet there is no doubt at all that it is the same species of butterfly, *Celastrina argiolus*, which is circum-polar, that is to say it occurs at these latitudes in all the corresponding areas around the globe. Later in the summer, the butterfly will be seen in numbers, feeding on the small sweet flowers of the cotoneaster, of which there is a veritable thicket in our front garden.

The Broad-leaf Maples are now in full flower, the long hanging racemes of yellow-green blossoms decorating every tree, each accompanied by a pair of still-unfolding five-lobed leaves, shapely emblems of our country (*Plate 13*). Before commencing my drawing, I took a couple of the individual flowers for a close examination, and was enthralled by the beauty of the structure. Five green petals and five green sepals curl together to form a neat inverted cup, from which ten long stamens protrude, encircling a forked pistil. Each stamen bears at its tip a dark-brown kidney-shaped anther, and the base of each stamen is covered with fine white bristles, which together form a soft "pappus" in the interior of the flower-cup, an altogether lovely arrangement. Some of the flowers had evidently been already pollinated, for the pistils had become lengthened and were withering, the ovaries already developing into the beginnings of those double-winged seeds that are such a familiar sight in early autumn, descending like miniature helicopters from every towering maple tree.

The Festal Day of Saint George, the dragon-slayer, patron of Olde *April 23* England! It was formerly my custom on St. George's Day to meet for luncheon with a dear lifelong friend, another loyal Canadian of English birth and traditions, each of us wearing a red rose, to drain a tankard in honour of the good Saint, the destroyer of Evil, the sworn enemy of Satan in his serpentine form. Alas, my dear friend Humphrey has gone to his rest, and toasting one's patron Saint is out of fashion and considered by many as "chauvinistic," whatever that nonsense-word may mean. But I can never glance at the calendar on April 23 without recalling, with some small nostalgia, our small private two-man ceremony. Humphrey had his own special name for the foaming draught we consumed on that occasion—the "pifflesnonker."

But this morning my attention was attracted to a tiny dragon-slayer of another kind. As I started out, I noticed that a paper-wasp had built a small neat nest under one of the projecting timber beams of our house, a perfectly symmetrical structure, about the size of a large duck egg, attached by its top to the undersurface of the beam, and with the top layer of the paper material projecting slightly and

COMMON AVENS
Geum macrophyllum

PLATE XII

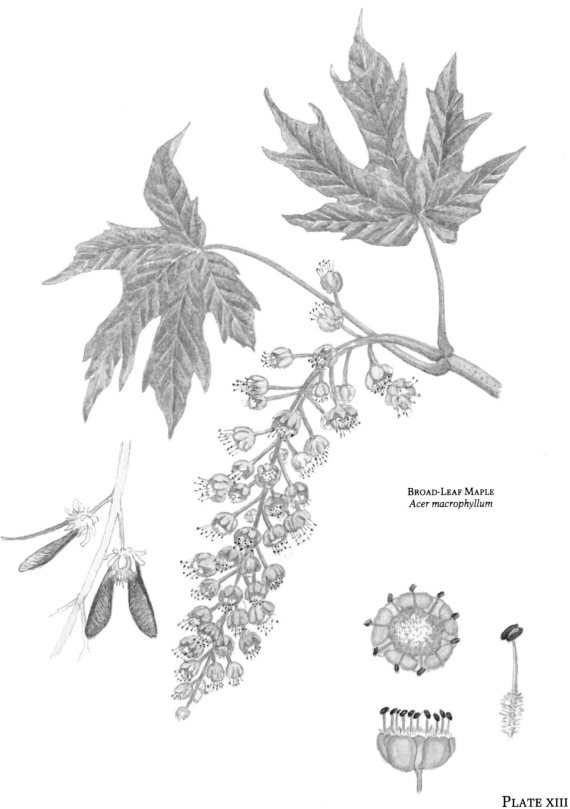

BROAD-LEAF MAPLE
Acer macrophyllum

PLATE XIII

overhanging the rest of the nest, possibly for the purpose of ventilation and temperature control, so important in the rearing of wasp-grubs, and perhaps representing the beginning of a new layer of the growing nest (*Plate 14*). A tiny hole, lead-pencil size, at the bottom tip of the cone, I noticed, was giving ingress and egress every few minutes to the owner-builder, one of the many species of paper-wasps which are a boon to gardeners and farmers in every land. I obtained a ladder and climbed up for a closer inspection of the little nest and, if possible, of its owner-occupant. The patience and industry with which these tiny creatures shave minute quantities of wood from the surfaces of fence posts and dead trees, and, mixing it with saliva, produce the fine paper material for their nests; this, and the perfection of the structure they make with it, are a never-failing source of wonder to me. This particular wasp appears to have obtained her raw material from two different sources, for she had built a two-tone nest, marbled prettily in two shades of gray and fawn. I found that attempting to manipulate a sketch pad and pencils at the top of a steeply-sloping ladder is a difficult, if not slightly risky undertaking. So instead, I went down for my camera and a close-range lens, hoping to secure a photograph or two from which to construct my drawing. My object was to trip the shutter at the exact moment of the insect's entry into or exit from the nest. But the busy wasp always flew an exact bee-line – or wasp-line – to the small entrance-hole and slipped in without an instant's hesitation. Her departure was always equally precipitous, and my reflexes, though good, were barely equal to the situation, and I fear the results of the effort, when the film is developed, may be somewhat less than satisfactory. But it will be interesting to watch and see what happens when the first lot of wasp-grubs are hatched into mature insects. Up to now, as far as I can tell, only one wasp, the queen, is going in and out, at intervals of about five minutes.

The common yellow-jacket wasp, which will be present in its legion later in the summer, is so far not much in evidence. For several weeks, at various points along my pedestrian route, I have noticed queen yellow-jackets blundering about among the rocks and tree-roots along the roadside, searching for some hole or fissure suitable for the establishment of a new colony. By now the new nests will all have been started, but the first lot of wasp-grubs, hatched from the first eggs laid by the queen and fed and tended by herself, will not yet have emerged as mature worker-wasps. When they do, they will take over the entire lifelong job of enlarging the excavation, building new layers of paper cells, and bringing home

food – chewed up caterpillars – for the new and future "litters" of wasp-grubs. Her Majesty will then remain in residence, and give herself over to her own lifelong job, the laying of several thousand eggs. Later in the summer she will die, doubtless of exhaustion, and this will be the signal for the colony to disperse. The worker-wasps will take a belated vacation among the late-summer flowers, helping themselves to any unharvested fruit, and making a nuisance of themselves around our picnic tables and patio tea parties. The newly-emerged females and drones will mate, and upon the first onset of winter weather, all will die except the fertilized females, next year's queens, who will find themselves secure crannies in which to pass the winter in hibernation. I have occasionally discovered a hibernating queen wasp in one of the deep clefts in the thick bark of a Douglas Fir tree, and am always surprised anew at what I see. During their active life, the wasps have six long, strong, and extremely active useful legs, supplied with strong claws, on which the insects walk and run (when not flying) and with which they manipulate food, earth, and building material with great skill. But in hibernation the queen takes a tight grip with her powerful jaws on the surface to which she has entrusted herself, and the wonderful jointed legs hang straight down, parallel with her body, and completely inactive throughout the long winter months, while she remains supported by her jaws alone.

But now, in April, this wonderful yearly life-cycle is but newly begun.

The bumblebee queens, too, have been bumbling about close to the ground along the roadside, they, like the yellow-jackets, looking for a place to start a new colony, albeit a very much less elaborate and refined establishment than that of the wasps. An abandoned mouse hole will suit Mrs. Bumble very nicely. Will redecorate to suit tenant.

It is noticeable that the buzzing tone of both the queen-wasp and the queen bumblebee is low, and the movements rather slow and leisurely. But it is early in the year, and the weather is cool. Since insects are "cold-blooded" animals, their metabolism slows down markedly in cold weather, and increases sharply when the days warm up. The buzzing sound is produced solely by the vibrating of the wings, and the pitch of the sound is low when the machinery that causes it is operating sluggishly. Wasps and bees do not "buzz angrily" as people often say, wrongly assigning human emotions to lesser creatures, but the sound rises sharply both in pitch and volume when the insect is disturbed, and slips into high gear in its need to move quickly.

FLOWERING DOGWOOD
Cornus nuttallii

PLATE XIV

PAPER-WASP
and early nest
Vespula sp.

BEACH PEA
Lathyrus japonicus

PLATE XV

April 27   This morning I walked again along the beach, and sat for a short space on a great log of driftwood, enjoying the warm sunshine. The sea was flat-calm and silvery blue, with a slight haze softening the outline of the distant hills of Vancouver Island. A great ship was lying at anchor a quarter of a mile from shore, and some sort of human activity taking place within her iron belly could be heard faintly, accentuating the quietness of a still morning, with no waves breaking, and, surprisingly, no keening from the gulls circulating and gyrating overhead.

A flotilla of eight small diving ducks – Buffleheads they seemed to be, though I saw them only in silhouette against the sun, and it was hard to be certain – were paddling along a few feet out from shore, making a seemingly leisurely journey from east to west. Every minute or so the lead duck up-tailed and disappeared below the surface of the sea, immediately followed by No. 2, then No. 3, and in very orderly fashion, one after another until all were gone. After about the length of time it took me to count ten slowly, up they popped again, one after another in the same orderly fashion; nothing at all haphazard about it, but all very smooth and well-regulated, as though something told them that any sort of disorderly behaviour would be out of keeping with a lovely, peaceful spring morning. They continued this manoeuvre at regular intervals until they were out of sight down the shore.

Close behind me where I sat, I noticed that the patch of Beach Pea was again sending up a dense growth of rich green multiple leaves, and several racemes of the flower-buds were showing the beginnings of the beautiful purple flowers (*Plate 15*). This particular legume grows right up out of the sea-sand where one would not expect to find nutriment for green and growing things.

April 30   Once again, today, I was walking in the rain. A very light rain, of the type commonly known as "Scotch mist." A tablecloth of light cloud is lying upon the mountainside and the highest point of my walk took me into the lower stratum of this cloud, so that I seemed to be enveloped in a bright atmosphere of minute droplets, hardly perceptible as falling rain, but capable of wetting me through in short order, were I not wearing a light nylon rain-shell, with a hood. For some strange reason, colours seemed to glow in this bright misty atmosphere. The Scotch Broom, so-called, is now at its best, and all along the rock-cut of the Upper Levels highway, and in many waste areas along the roadside, the bushes, densely laden with the golden blossoms, add a special charm to the morning.

The Broom is another uncommonly hardy immigrant from the Old World, which has found this new habitat very much to its liking. There are a number of conflicting explanations as to how it got here, none susceptible of proof. Although it is generally known in this country as "Scotch Broom" it is by no means exclusively Scottish in origin, but is a common shrub throughout much of western Europe, including France. It has been placed by taxonomists in a genus *Cytisis*, and given the specific name *scoparius*, Latin for "broom," though I do not know whether it would be suitable for sweeping the patio, or if it has, historically, been so used. But the old classical name by which the Romans knew it is *genista. Planta genista*—"a sprig of Broom." In the twelfth century, Count Geoffry of Anjou adopted this "sprig of Broom" as a family emblem. His son Henry of Anjou succeeded him to the title; but Henry, through his mother, was a grandson of King Henry I of England and upon the death in 1154 of the English King Stephen, became the natural successor to the throne of England. So, in good order, and complete with his family emblem of the *Planta genista*, he became King Henry II Plantagenet, first of that noble dynasty.

In the early nineteenth century, the Rev. Richard Harris Barham recorded this in the delightful, hilarious doggerel of the "Ingoldsby Legends"—on which, thanks to my father, I was brought up:

> We're all aware that on the throne there once sat
> A very great King with an Angevin hat,
> And a fine Sprig of Broom that he wore as a badge in it,
> And was named from that circumstance, Henry Plantagenet!

Henry II was indeed a very great king, but alas, his talents as a ruler and administrator, so valuable to a turbulent England, are often less remembered than his alleged responsibility for the murder, in Canterbury Cathedral, of his erstwhile friend and chancellor, the good St. Thomas à Becket. How little could this mediaeval monarch have guessed that the yellow shrub of his boyhood, and emblem of his kingship, would one day glorify the mountain slopes of a continent yet undreamed of by Europeans of his day!

When the sun is shining, and the weather warmer than it has been today, I can never pass a broom bush in full flower without pausing for a few minutes in the hope of seeing a honey-bee perform its special pollination trick on the bright yellow flowers. Like the blossoms of all Legumes, the flower has one of its petals arranged as a broad "banner" standing erect at the base; two more extending as "wings" at the sides, and two others joined together as a sort of "keel" or boat, in which the stamens and pistil are contained. The keel is closed along its upper edge by a weak seam, and, as the flower develops, the stamens and pistil within grow longer and curl up into a kind of watch-spring formation. When a bee visits the blossom seeking nectar, she pushes down with her long proboscis on the weak seam, the keel splits open and the stamens and pistil spring up over the bee's back (*Plate 16*). The pistil collects some of the pollen from a previously-visited flower, while the stamens anoint the bee with some of their own pollen, to be carried to still another blossom, thus ensuring a modicum of cross-pollination, to the benefit of the species. But should the particular blossom not be blessed by a bee, the lengthening stamens and pistil will eventually cause the keel to split open by itself and allow them to come into contact with each other so that self-pollination, though less beneficial to the species than cross-pollination, will take place, a sort of second line of defence.

But this morning it was cool and wet, the sun was not shining, and no bees were in evidence. The rain, however, does not seem to dampen the spirits of the feathered fraternity. Our summer resident birds are arriving in great numbers, as well as many migrants on their way through, heading generally north. I noticed this morning many of the large and beautiful Band-tailed Pigeons flying about the treetops, the broad white borders across the fanned-out tail showing momentarily as they "air-braked" for a landing on some high branch. The air seemed full of their soft cooing call.

SCOTCH BROOM
Cytisus scoparius

THIMBLEBERRY
Rubus parviflorus

PLATE XVI

May

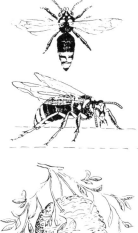

May 1 The Flowering Dogwood is now approaching its fullest development, a May phenomenon to which all dwellers in this coastal area look forward. But alas, this is apparently not a gala year for the Dogwood. These "off" years do sometimes happen, and instead of the many Dogwood trees along my pedestrian route appearing as dense masses of white, this year the blossoms are quite spottily dispersed over the trees. Indeed, not only in quantity but also in quality, this year the Dogwoods are poor, and I was even hard put to it this morning, to select a reasonably handsome spray of blossoms and leaves from which to make my drawing. The very opposite is the case with the Scotch Broom, the bushes of which are everywhere more densely clothed in golden yellow than I have ever before seen them.

The wasps' nest under the roof beam is progressing mightily. What was, but a week ago, as I reported, about the size of a duck egg, is now a good sized grapefruit. The overhanging cape of the paper shell was, indeed, the beginning of a new layer, which has now been completed and two or three more added. Each new layer has a small entrance hole, lined up with the hole in the previous layer, so that there must now be the beginning of a tunnel from the outside to the centre, where the egg-laying queen is enthroned. The workers are now going in and out of the aperture in considerable numbers, carrying food to the queen and to a fresh brood of wasp-grubs, and several wasps can be seen on the outer surface of the growing nest, adding minute quantities of paper pulp to the edge of the newest layer, as it progresses from the top downwards.

The gardens and the roadsides where I walk are now alive with robin families, the spotted-breasted youngsters already as big as their parents, chirping in a demanding manner to be fed, though they are long since fully fledged, and well able to fend for themselves.

May 6 Today I walked somewhat further afield than my usual selection of routes along the surrounding thoroughfares, for I was invited to join, as an elderly guide and commentator, a quite charming group of

54

young matrons, some of them school teachers, at a nature rendezvous in nearby Lighthouse Park, a 185-acre parcel of virgin-forested land occupying the promontory of Atkinson Point, some two miles from my home. This is a small surviving piece of the Forest Primeval, having been, for a number of sound historic reasons, preserved from devastation by commercial logging, and from subdivision for residential development like the—admittedly lovely—area surrounding it on three sides. As a result, the hardy vegetable invaders from overseas have made but limited inroads into the park, and the more delicate native plants can be found here growing in their natural forest habitat. This situation is beloved of our local amateur botanists who are apt to become quite nationalistic about "British Columbia Flowers," tending to scorn the imported "weeds" and to treat these often quite beautiful invading plants with a disdain which I, personally, do not share.

Nevertheless, the native plants, growing sometimes in the shadow of the great fir and cedar trees, and sometimes on the sun-shafted slopes of the granite outcrops, have a delicate beauty of their own, and efforts to prevent their being over-run by intruders are entirely commendable. The season is late, for the recent preponderance of cool, wet weather has set the growth at least two, and perhaps three weeks behind its normal schedule. The vigorous and sharp-eyed young women were able to find an occasional "Fawn-lily" (*Erythronium oreganum*)—still in flower, which should have passed long ago into the seed-pod stage. One or two plants of the *Zygadene*, or "Death-Camas" were also to be found growing in soil-filled clefts in the rocks along the shore. But the flower sprays of the Salal, which should by now be showing the first signs of their pale shell-pink bells, are still only tight green buds. We were, however, rewarded in several places by finding patches of that other member of the great heather family, the Bear-berry, which the Coast Indians call *Kinnick-kinnick*, and which always moves the nature lover to exclamations of delight with its glossy green leaves and rose-pink bell flowers. Bears are known to be addicted to berries, a fact which tends to become recorded in the botanical names of berry-bearing plants. I observed earlier in this journal that the Blackberry has been named *Rubus ursinus*, from *Ursa*, Latin for bear. Likewise, the *Kinnick-kinnick* has been placed in a genus of its own called *Arctostictos* from *Arctos*, Greek for bear, and given a specific name, *Uva-ursi*, literally, "Bear-berry."

A great place, this Lighthouse Park, and a priceless asset to this North Shore community. The prestigious Vancouver Natural

History Society, in its project to make a general survey of the natural species peculiar to nearby coastal regions, chose Lighthouse Park as an entirely representative yet very compact study area, and has entitled the resulting popular book *Nature West Coast as Seen in Lighthouse Park*.

But today the weather did not choose to co-operate and, though the company was charming, the occasion, as a Nature Walk, was something less than productive. A further visit in a few weeks' time, when the beautiful Columbia Lilies are lifting their bright orange heads, may be more rewarding.

May 12   As I stepped out of the house this morning, I was arrested by a familiar sound emanating from the old cedar tree which grows on the rock slope just across the road. It was one of those rather rare moments of complete quiet; no traffic sound from Marine Drive, no train approaching on the nearby railway line, no airplane passing overhead. But the "chunk-chunk-chunk" from across the road, which might have been lost among those other man-made sounds, was familiar and unmistakable – the chiselling of a Pileated Woodpecker. For many years now, almost as long as we have lived in this house, one of these large and spectacular birds has, at unpredictable and rather long intervals, and at all seasons of the year, visited this same poor old cedar tree which though apparently still living, is riddled with the great oblong holes made by the woodpecker's sharp chisel beak. Why the tree has not long since come down in one of our spirited Westerlies, I do not know. But it lives on, its riven heart still evidently harbouring enough beetle-grubs to render the visits of the Pileated Woodpecker worthwhile.

The chisel-beak does its work with rapidly-repeated blows, powered by the long muscular neck, and the big chips of bark and wood fly in all directions. At other times the bird taps tentatively and lightly, apparently exploring by sound the situation below the surface.

These visits have been going on, from time to time, for many more years than I think can possibly represent the normal life-span of a Pileated Woodpecker. But I suffer from the illusion that it is the same individual bird revisiting a well-remembered source of nourishment, and it has become, to me, a sort of friend. It seems reasonably tame, and does not appear to resent my close approach. At least it does not fly off when I appear. But it does, most tantalizingly, retire to the far side of the cedar trunk to resume its operations where I cannot see it, occasionally cocking its head, with flaring red pileus and beady black eye, around one side or the other, no doubt to check up on my intentions.

Normally, it starts at the bottom of the tree, and ascends in a spiral path, thereby ultimately covering the whole surface of the lower twenty feet or so of the trunk in its explorations. During parts of the manoeuvre it is, of course, in clear view, often with the sun shining on its brilliant black, white and red plumage, an arresting sight. I have been trying for years to obtain motion-pictures of the infuriating bird, but as soon as I approach close enough to obtain a good sized image, even with a long-focus telephoto lens, it retires behind the tree trunk, periodically peering around at me with an expression which, in a human, would be an impudent grin. Damn the rascal!

May 15

The roadside banks and ditches are now a green jungle of growing plants, gay with flowers of which the predominating colour is yellow. The common lawn dandelion, bane of gardeners everywhere, is now past its first spring explosion of yellow flower-heads, and the wonderful globular seed-heads, the children's "dandelion clocks," are everywhere to be seen. In an absurd impulse of remembered childhood, I picked one of these, and blew on it as many times as was necessary to divest it of all its tiny seed parachutes, thus establishing that it was five o'clock. My quartz-digital watch, however, usually considered more reliable, failed to confirm this, and I was forced, by weight of other circumstances, to conclude that it was actually half past nine.

The dandelions' method of spreading their seed abroad by wind action, a method shared by many plants of the composite order, is always a source of great wonderment to me. The beauty of the tiny seed-achenes, the method of their development, and the geometrical perfection of their attachment to the cushioned head of the plant-stem, are a delight to behold, as is the gorgeous beauty of the dandelion flower-head itself. It is a pity that the great rosettes of jagged-edged green leaves are such a disfigurement to a tidy lawn, and that the deep tap-roots, once established, are so difficult to eradicate. The French compared the deeply-indented leaves to lions' teeth, and called the plant *dents-de-lion*, whence our common name.

But today, more abundant than the lawn dandelion was the native tall "Hairy Cat's-ear," a related but only superficially similar species. The similarly shaped leaves are thick and hairy, and the bright yellow flower-heads, somewhat smaller than those of the lawn dandelion, are carried high on rather graceful, tall, branched stems.

PLATE XVII

SUMMER GRASSES

WESTERN TIGER SWALLOWTAIL
Papilio rutulus

CLOUDY PARNASSIAN
Parnassus clodias

PLATE XVIII

They are present now in great numbers, and together with the myriad golden cups of the common buttercup, are making a brave show along the roadsides.

The grasses, too, thanks presumably to the very unusual amount of rain, are in a very lush condition along the borders of the road (*Plate 17*). I counted at least four separate species this morning, although I have not identified them as to their botanical kind, but all are now in bloom, lifting their many-flowered heads high on long graceful stalks. One in particular which even in its sere brown condition in January captivated me and led me to make a drawing of it, is now fresh-sprung and vivid green, the flower-stalks standing almost seven feet tall. In passing this morning I paused to examine some of the tiny individual green flowers with a small but powerful hand-lens I always carry with me. The flowers are somewhat bizarre in form, but similar among the different species in their general arrangement – a green sheath from which protrude two feather-like pistils and three stamens, their anthers quivering on threadlike filaments. Some are already making seed, and the wealth of tall grass flowers, standing high above the general level of the greenery, give the appearance of a greenish-purple mist as they move gently in the sea breeze.

May 21 Once again, a warm sunny day, though the weatherman, dismal fellow, gives us no promise of its long continuance. But the butterflies are taking advantage of the summer-like day. I am sure they must have been feeling frustrated by the cool wet weather, when no butterfly flies. This morning one of our big Tiger Swallowtails appeared, soaring over the blackberry thicket, which is now beginning to display its annual snowstorm of white blossom. This was one of the so-called "Pale Tiger Swallowtails" known to lepidopterists as *Papilio eurymedon*. It carries the black and yellow coloration peculiar to all except one of the North American Swallowtails. But in the case of this *P. eurymedon* the yellow is paled down to a creamy white, and the black tiger-stripes are very broad and bold. This great butterfly always seems to appear earlier in the year than the much commoner "Western Tiger Swallowtail," whose markings are similar, but whose colouring is a clear bright lemon-yellow in between the characteristic black tiger-stripes (*Plate 18*).

I also, today, caught sight of a Western White Admiral, or "Lorquin's Admiral" sunning its glossy wings as it rested on the leaf of a maple sapling. Like all the "White Admirals" this insect has jet-black wings, each pair crossed by a broad bar of purest white. On the outer front corner, or "apical angle" of each forewing it bears a short border of orange-brown, showing its family relationship to a group of other butterflies of the same genus in which orange-brown and black are predominating colours. The White Admiral of the eastern part of the continent does not bear this orange birthmark, but instead has a border on the hind-wings of sky-blue crescents. Both these "Admirals" carry on the underside of the wings a remarkable jazz-pattern of tawny orange, black, white and gray in spots, and bars which produce a strongly "cryptic" effect, rendering the insect very difficult to see when at rest with the wings folded together, whereas it is highly visible when the striking black-and-white upper surfaces are extended in the sunshine.

The English common names for butterflies are interesting, and sometimes poetic. It would be interesting to know where they all come from. Scientific names, using Latin or Greek (or a hodge-podge of the two) have been bestowed by scholars in the field, and there has been just as much argument and squabbling among the learned, about the proper assignment of these scientific names, as in most other fields of natural history. Carl Linne (*Carolus Linnaeus*, the father of systematic taxonomy) knew of only about one hundred different species of butterflies, and put them all into one genus, which he called *Papilio*, Latin for butterfly. Being also a classical scholar, for specific or individual names, he turned, picturesquely, to beings of the world of mythology, thus, *Papilio ajax, P. agamemnon*, and so on. Many of these mythological names, happily, still survive, but with more than twenty thousand different species of butterflies now known throughout the world, other, and more logical sources of nomenclature, both generic and specific, have had to be adopted. Often these consist of a brief word of a descriptive nature in Latin or latinized Greek; and not infrequently, the name of the original discoverer or describer of the species, rendered into the Latin genitive form, thus, *Limenitis lorquinii*, Lorquin's Admiral, from Lorquin, the naturalist who first listed the insect in official records (*Plate 19*).

But the common names in English are often strange and incomprehensible. Why "admiral," for there is also a Red Admiral, belonging to a totally different genus. One writer has opined that the word was formerly "admirable." The "White Admirable Butterfly"? It does not sound too plausible. And there is a large group of tropical Asiatic butterflies named (by English-speaking naturalists of the area) "Shoemakers," I have not the least glimmer of an idea why! Some butterflies, more reasonably, have received common English

SALMONBERRY
Rubus spectabilis

LORQUIN'S ADMIRAL
Limenitis lorquinii

PLATE XIX

NARROW-LEAVED PLANTAIN
Plantago lanceolata

PLATE XX

names descriptive of their colours, or of the food-plant of their caterpillars, or both; thus, the Cabbage White, the Holly Blue, the Meadow Brown, the Clouded Yellow, and so forth.

But biology is a universal science, and these same butterflies, occurring in other countries, have other sets of names in other languages. Thus it is the only practical and sensible method of rendering worldwide study possible, and discussion available to all, to make use of the so-called "dead" languages of Latin and classical Greek, with which all serious scholars are supposed to be familiar. It is a solution which works well, even though the taxonomists sometimes take outrageous liberties with these sonorous historic tongues.

May 26 The Thimbleberry bushes are now coming into full flower, appearing here and there among the thickets of bramble-blackberry, a member of the same genus, *Rubus*. The fine white five-petalled blossoms, growing in groups of five or six at the end of the leaf-stems are never slightly pink-tinted, as the blackberry flowers sometimes are, but are always purest white. They call to my memory yet another member of the *Rubus* clan, the Flowering Raspberry, which was familiar to me, growing along the roadsides in Eastern Canada. The two plants are almost identical in form, but the Eastern species called (for obvious reasons) *Rubus odorata*, has flowers of rose-pink. Our white flowered Thimbleberry is named *Rubus parviflorus*, "small flowered" or "few-flowered," which I find somewhat puzzling, for the handsome white blossoms are regularly larger, and no less abundant than those of our other two common *Rubus* species, the common trailing Blackberry and the equally ubiquitous Salmonberry, *Rubus spectabilis* ("showy"). The Salmonberry, which was cheering us with its rose-red flowers in blustery March and wet April, is now displaying its luscious-looking, but gastronomically disappointing fruit. Starting as tight green berries nestling in the calyxes of the withered flowers, these fruits have passed through a stage of bright gamboge-yellow colouring, to the rich carmine red of the ripe Salmonberry, still sitting in the five-pointed calyx and surrounded by a dense halo of dark red stamens, beautiful to see and a pleasure to draw and paint.

All along the road-edge, the Narrow-leaved Plantain is sending up bunches of tall stems bearing the strange white flowers (*Plate 20*). The cone-shaped bud, surrounded by a coronet of tiny white florets always calls to my mind the headdress of an Oriental Vizier in an illustration in my old copy of the *Arabian Nights*. The rings of flower-buds come into bloom progressively from the bottom to the top of the bud, so that, below the ring currently in blossom, there is always a mass of brownish dead or dying florets, and above it a number of neat rings of bud-lets still waiting to flower. The plant is actually a pernicious weed, though perhaps not quite so persistent as its close relative the Broad-leaved Plantain, which infests our lawns and crushed-stone driveways.

The busy wasps' nest, which was a duck egg when I first reported it, and shortly became a grapefruit, is now a sizeable football, and I fear I shall soon have to get rid of it before the wasps start to become a nuisance to us and our garden visitors. I am very reluctant to disturb the wasps, for their industry fascinates me, and they are, up to now, peaceable and mild-tempered little creatures. I have been watching them, on several occasions, perched on the top of a ladder only a few inches from the nest, and they come and go about their urgent affairs, taking no notice of me whatsoever. Their nest is a work of art!

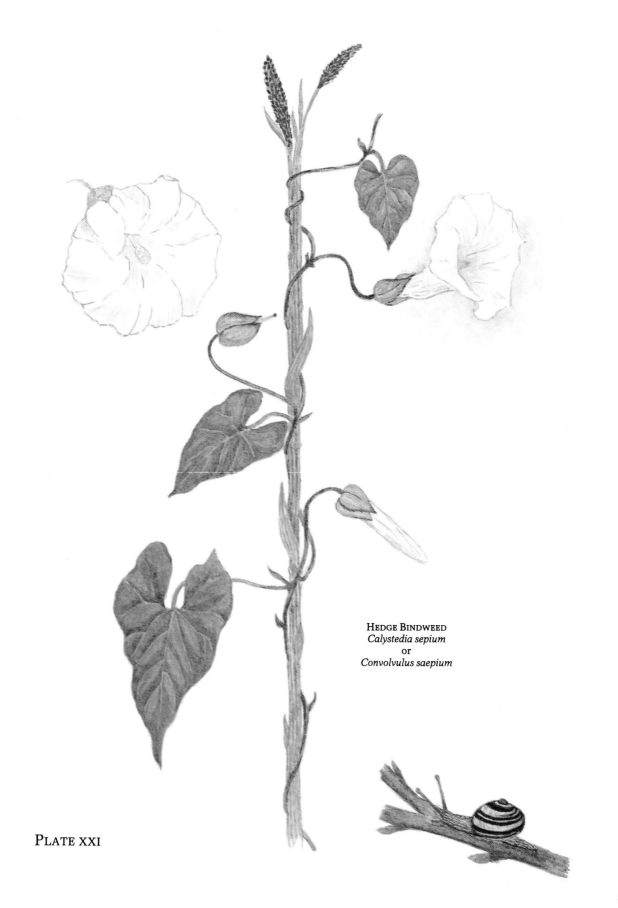

HEDGE BINDWEED
Calystedia sepium
or
Convolvulus saepium

PLATE XXI

June

Our somewhat backward, cool and wet spring does not seem to have proved any hardship to green and growing things in this lush coastal area, especially the "weeds" – those unfortunate and vigorous plants which are unlucky enough to be growing where human residents choose not to want them. The bushes along the roadsides are now becoming richly over-run with the ubiquitous Hedge Bindweed. The handsome heart-shaped leaves on the rapidly-growing tendrils are already completely covering some of the common shrubs, and the landscape seems to be richly dotted with the great white trumpets of the Bindweed blossom – a delicately beautiful plant though a persistent weed, a bane to gardeners everywhere. There is a common, though quite incorrect notion, based upon common lack of accurate observation, that climbing plants like the Bindweed achieve their spiral growth by following the daily circling of the sun. This particular plant gives the lie to that notion, for it always twists in a counter-clockwise motion (viewed in the direction of growth), the tendency to do so being evidently pre-programmed into the genes of the plant, while the reverse is true of some other species. In the words of one of those witty and catching songs written and performed by Flanders and Swan:

> The fragrant Honeysuckle spirals clockwise to the sun,
> And many other creepers do the same.
> But some climb anti-clockwise – the Bindweed does for one –
> Or *Convolvulus*, to give her proper name!

Con-Volvulus – a "twisting together." The Bindweed lives amply up to this generic name. The young plants, rising from the ground as seedlings, gather together a bunch of grass-stems, and spiraling around them, bind them together into a stout fascia up which the Bindweed lifts itself in search of more stable support in the surrounding bushes (*Plate 21*). Before the end of the summer many of these bushes will be completely covered and almost hidden by the broad leaves, which are intermediate in shape between the two forms botanically known as *cordate* (heart-shaped) and *sagitate* (arrowhead-shaped). But the leaves arrange themselves, face-up, in the most graceful of patterns, with but little overlapping, but in such a manner as to completely cover the supporting bush below.

There seems, just now, to be an unusual increase in the number of snails from what we normally expect. As I took my walk this morning I seemed to see the small brown prettily-marked shells everywhere; on the wayside flower-stalks, on the rocks, climbing up the stems of the maple saplings, and sometimes on the ground at my feet. Doing some much-needed clearing and thinning in the garden yesterday, we removed an overgrown bush of ornamental white broom, and found a conclave of twenty or more of these small molluscs clustered about the main stem, close to the base. It is interesting to observe the wide variation in colouring of the shells of these little creatures; always in shades of brown, from light tan to dark chestnut, there seems an endless variety in the number and shades in the bands of colour surrounding the shell, parallel to its whorls. The animal is commonly known as the "Faithful Snail" – why, I do not know; possibly a simple translation from the Latin of its scientific name, *Monodenia fidelis*, but the only evidence of fidelity of which I am aware is, perhaps, that it can be faithfully depended upon to make serious depredations upon small garden seedlings if its numbers are not controlled, for, like its cousin the black slug, it can be a serious menace in this respect.

June 6 This morning, on my walk up the mountainside in a bright glow of morning sun, I was "buzzed" twice by a Rufous Hummingbird, suspended momentarily on rapidly vibrating wings a few feet in front of my face and scrutinizing me carefully with a minute beady eye (*Plate 22*). A few of these feathered jewels stay with us through the winter, thanks no doubt to bird-lovers who provide them with sugar solution in regular Hummingbird feeders built to resemble flowers. But it is always the sudden profusion of bright flowers in our June gardens which causes the tiny, brilliant birds to appear in numbers. While they visit almost any nectar-rich blossoms, the colour red seems to attract them more than any other, and beds of scarlet geraniums seem to be especially favoured. It is a fascinating sight to watch a hummingbird feeding at a plant having long tubular flowers, like the *Kniphofia* ("Red-hot Poker"). The bird hangs on rapidly-beating wings below the down-hanging flower-tubes, and pushes its long slender bill upward into the flower, its still longer sticky tongue probing for the nectar and for the minute insects often also present. I seem to see female hummingbirds much more often

than the males. Both sexes have grayish bellies and iridescent metallic green backs and wing-coverts. Only the males have the rich rufous colouring of the breast and the brilliant scarlet collar, and those are only at their best during the mating season. Occasionally, individuals of two other species, Anna's Hummingbird and the Black-chinned Hummingbird are recorded in this area, but I have not seen them here, and ornithological friends assure me that only the Rufous Hummingbird nests and breeds in this north coastal region of North America.

A few years ago, we were greatly privileged to have a pair of these lovely little creatures build their nest, a superb structure of lichen, moss, and cobwebs, in a hanging cedar branch just outside our front door, and raise their family of three bumble-bee-sized infants in full view of our spare bedroom window (*Plate 23*). The nests are usually very hard to detect, resembling as they do a knot or protuberance on the branch of a tree. Hummingbirds, despite their small size, have the reputation of being the most pugnacious and quarrelsome of all birds.

June is the month of the Swallowtail butterflies, and this morning, *June 15* on my way down to the shore to take advantage of the low tide for a walk along the beach, I caught sight of more than one of the big yellow fellows, sailing high among the trees and very visible against the dark foliage of the Douglas Firs. They love the white blossoms of the ever-present blackberry vines, and are also especially attracted to the heady sweetness of the *Philadelphus*, or (incorrectly so-called) *Syringa*, or "Mock Orange." We have two of these fine flowering shrubs in the garden, and just today a specially fine specimen of the Tiger Swallowtail (*Papilio rutulus*) was busily sucking up the sweet nectar, apparently to some degree intoxicated by its orgy, as is not infrequently the case with certain butterflies on certain flowers.

At any rate, I was able to approach and examine it at close range, and could probably have taken it with my bare thumb and finger, had I so desired, so little did it seem to be concerned by my presence. I noticed, however, that its perfection was somewhat marred by the loss of one of its long black "tails," with which the hind wings are graced, giving the genus its popular name. There is a theory regarding the purpose of these tails, and certain other types of characteristic decoration on the wings of butterflies. It is suggested that, when the insect is in flight, these excrescences form a natural target for birds pursuing it as prey for food, and will serve to deflect the predator's attention from more vital parts of the butterfly's body.

RUFOUS HUMMING-BIRD
Selasphorus rufus

FEMALE ♀

MALE ♂

IMMATURE ♂ MALE

FEMALE ♀

PLATE XXII

Inside diameter of cup 1⅜"
Outside diameter of nest 2⅜"
Depth ¼"

NEST OF RUFOUS HUMMING-BIRD
(from life, natural size)

PLATE XXIII

A small snippet, or even a substantial portion, or a tail, lost from a wing does not greatly discommode a butterfly, though admittedly spoiling its perfection from the human point of view. The theory would seem to be well-founded, for collectors complain that it is difficult to obtain a specimen of the Swallowtail in the wild with both tails intact, and it is in fact common to find butterflies, of many species, with small pieces missing from the hind-wing, pieces having shapes suspiciously suggestive of a bird's beak.

I have so far been unsuccessful in finding, on my walks abroad, one of the rather spectacular caterpillars of this fine butterfly, which I should like to draw from life, and I have found it necessary to work from colour-slides presented to me by that indefatigable naturalist and wildlife photographer, Enid Lemon, of Victoria, British Columbia. If one is lucky, however, one may sometimes find one of the remarkably-coloured "worms" among the leaves of maple, cherry or other of the several food plants favoured by the species; or, occasionally, one may spot a female *Papilio* in the momentary act of laying one of her minute globular green eggs on the underside of a leaf, and the egg can then be taken home and bred through the four stages of metamorphosis to the mature butterfly. More often than not, however, the butterflies fly, and do their egg-laying and the caterpillars feed, among the higher branches of the food trees where they are well out of reach of casual observers, particularly those of the Quiet Pedestrian variety. But the rearing of a butterfly, through the four stages from egg to "imago" by the simple expedient of providing a sheltered place of confinement and a continuing supply of fresh food plant, is a rewarding, and to some a profoundly moving experience. Some claim to see, in the emergence of the mature butterfly from its larval and pupal states, a parallel to the release of the human spirit from the bondage of the flesh, and find beauty in the metaphor. To me this is entirely fallacious and rather silly. I do not need mystical mumbo-jumbo to help me to appreciate the wonder of these small miracles of the world of nature.

June 18   This morning, once again taking the Upper Road for my walk, I caught sight, somewhat to my surprise, of another butterfly of the same family (*Papilionidae*) as the Swallowtail tribe, but one without tails and very different in appearance; this was a "Smoky Parnassian" (*Parnassus clodias*). The name of the genus *Parnassus* once more exemplifies Carl Linne's penchant for the classics, and the beings and places of Greek mythology. For the members of this genus of butterflies are all insects of the mountain valleys and high Alpine

meadows where the caterpillars of most, if not all of the species feed on the various kinds of *Sedum* (Stonecrop) or, occasionally, Saxifrage, both plants characteristic of the windy heights. Our "Smoky Parnassian" is a fairly common insect in some years in its normal habitat, but it seldom descends to the lower levels, and thus to see it along the roadside even at the most elevated points of my daily peregrinations is, to me, always something of an "occasion," though I have, it is true, once or twice seen a specimen flitting about in our own garden, only a hundred feet or so above sea level. An unusual looking butterfly with creamy-white semi-transparent wings, rounded in shape, with darker markings of smoky-gray and a number of predominant spots, black and orange-red, on both the upper and the lower surfaces. I can never see one of these butterflies without thinking of the "Apollo"–(*Linnaeus* and his mythology again!)–undoubtedly the best-known species of the genus, which is found in the high meadows of the European Alps. It was once a too-common practice for tourists hiking or climbing in Switzerland to bring home specimens of the Apollo butterfly which, like a sprig of Edelweiss served as a sort of trophy brought from the high places. As with the Edelweiss, this practice has now been stopped, and both the plant and the butterfly have been placed by the Swiss government on the "protected" list. I hope this action will not become necessary for the welfare of our charming little *Parnassus clodias*, the smoky one.

With great regret, I found it advisable last night to destroy the wasps' nest which I had been watching with interest and amusement for so many days, for it had grown to the size of a football, and the queen's horde of industrious progeny have been streaming in and out, enlarging the wonderful paper structure layer by layer and bringing morsels of food for the maturing wasp-grubs within (*Plate 24*). But I can no longer subject my summer visitors and patio guests to the growing hazard of a painful sting. So, waiting until the last rays of light were dying from the western sky, so that all the wasps would be "home" in the nest for the night, and feeling rather like a murderous ogre, I climbed the ladder, listening to the sleepy murmur inside the nest, and placed over the complete structure a big paper bag (from the local supermarket), having first placed within it a large cotton swab soaked with acetone, the vapours of which are lethal to most insects. The upper edges of the paper bag I taped to the supporting roof beams, to render the "gas chamber" both air-tight and wasp-tight. Then I retired to bed, leaving the whole edifice intact for

June 25

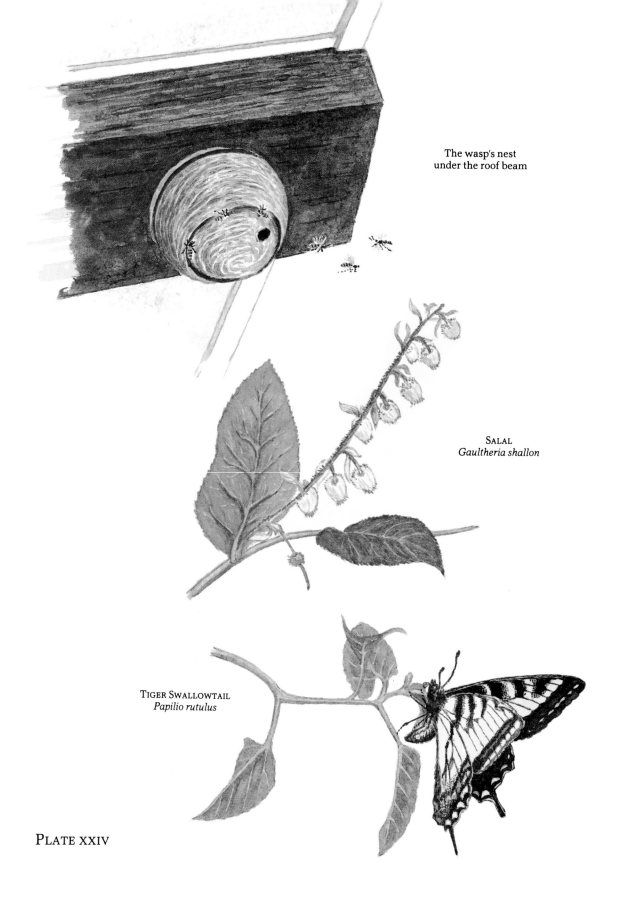

The wasp's nest
under the roof beam

Salal
Gaultheria shallon

Tiger Swallowtail
Papilio rutulus

Plate XXIV

the acetone to do its work as mercifully as possible. And that is where I made my big mistake.

Perhaps the acetone-soaked swab was not big enough; peradventure I should not have waited all night for the next step—the cutting down and burning of the defunct colony. At all events, this morning I once more ascended the ladder with a large butcher knife and started to slice along the lower surface of the beam to which the nest was attached, intending that the nest and its dead occupants should simply fall into the bag and be put quickly to the torch. Unfortunately, a not-inconsiderable number of the wasps had failed to succumb to the fumes, or, more probably had recovered from their asphyxia during the cool hours of night after the acetone had all evaporated, and I was promptly confronted with a large cloud of very bewildered wasps, buzzing in a puzzled manner about the place where the nest with its queen should be, but no longer was. I was then subjected to a striking demonstration, if such were needed, of the apparently complete lack of reasoning power, or any sense of cause-and-effect, in these otherwise clever-seeming little animals. I left them alone, assuming that, deprived of the magnet attraction of the nest and its queen, they would drift off among the garden flowers, as normally happens when the queen dies naturally of old age in the autumn. But this residue of the wasp colony, after the first bewildered frenzy had subsided, gathered again in a quivering mass on the surface of the beam where the nest had been, as though conferring about the possibility of repairing the damage. Some blind impulse seemed to have told them that something very improperly had become uncovered, and should be covered up again as soon as possible. It will be interesting to see what, if anything, happens in the next few days. Will they attempt to build more new cells? There is no queen now to lay eggs with which to fill the cells, and their work, if it continues, will be for nothing!

Dogs! I would not ordinarily expect to include these engaging *June 30* quadrupeds in a Nature Diary, but they not infrequently become an integral part of my customary pedestrianism. We are not, at the moment, owned by a dog, and have not been for a good many years. But I like dogs, and they have an uncanny way of knowing this, so that quite often, on my walk, I experience that strange sense of "presence" that one so often encounters, and, looking around, find that I am accompanied by a friendly canine. I do not encourage this, in fact I go to some length in trying to discourage the animals from following me on my daily walks, but it is not always easy, for they can be very persistent. Sometimes I will find myself speaking very sternly to some attractive brown-eyed spaniel, ordering it in my severest tones to "stay home, now; *stay home!*" And the dog will stare back at me with that hurt expression that only a nice dog knows how to assume, making me feel a heartless curmudgeon. I turn and walk on for fifty yards, look back, and see the deeply offended animal still staring balefully at me. I turn again and resume my walk for a further fifty yards when – that feeling again! – I look behind me, and there is Towzer nonchalantly trotting along at my heels. For who knows better than an artful dog that the Dumb Walking Man is in reality a softie, a pushover?! Sometimes I may have three or four assorted canines escorting me on my way, and often one or more will accompany me all the way back to my house, and again stare at me with that scandalized look when not allowed to come in for a visit. And I worry lest they be unable to find their way home, though they usually seem to do so.

But it is wrong in principle. We have local bylaws forbidding dogs to be at large, unaccompanied, on the streets – which rules are far too often ignored and flouted. A dog with its unquestioning love and devotion gives us much, and is entitled to something more in exchange than mere shelter and victuals. For, unlike a cat, a dog longs for human companionship far more than for food and shelter, and a walk in company with a human friend is a dog's highest form of pleasure. I am convinced that if every dog-owner could bring him or herself, every morning and every evening, to perform the simple unselfish task of giving his canine friend a regular walk – a *real* walk, not just fifty yards up the road to defecate on someone else's lawn – the dog, knowing it could with faith and confidence look forward to this session with its favourite human, would stay happily indoors or in its kennel during the day and never succumb to the itch to follow a stranger. But my daily walk takes me past many an affluent-looking residence whose open empty double garage doors reveal that both grownups are away at work, the children at school, and a lonely dog put outside to fend for itself. If I were such a dog – particularly one of the nice animals with which I have become friendly – I am sure that nothing would deter me from attaching myself to that Quiet Pedestrian who so regularly passes by!

July

Dominion Day—Canada Day, what you will, but the 114th anniversary of the federation of the first group of the provinces of this lovely land, and thus Canada's 114th birthday, an annual public holiday, and a glorious sunny day to boot! As I took my morning walk along the beach, the sea at half-tide, the holiday sailors were already out in numbers, their argosies of white or brightly-coloured sails standing well out in a surface-wrinkling breeze. The wind was fresh during the night, but has now subsided to some extent, and the receding tide has left a line of minor jetsam along the beach. A thin tangle of seaweed lay along the high-water line, consisting chiefly of the olive-brown Rockweed, doubtless torn from the nearby boulders, but here and there interspersed with a bright green ribbon of sea-cabbage and an occasional long whiplash of the strange Bull Kelp, floated in on the tide from some more distant place. The shoreline here consists of a sloping beach of large and small water-worn boulders lying on a base of clean quartz sand, and the marine life to be found here is of the type normally inhabiting such a beach. We do not, in this vicinity boast many of the wonderful tide pools—natural marine aquariums—that display a fascinating variety of sea creatures in some other areas of this coast. Also, oceanographers tell me that, because of the effect of the great Fraser River which pours itself into the sea just beyond the jutting eminence of Point Grey, added to that of the many mountain streams that tumble into the bay along this north shore, the salinity of the seawater is somewhat lower here than that along the open ocean, and the variety and type of the sea life on this beach is further affected and controlled by that circumstance. But the boulders within the tidal limits are liberally encrusted with acorn-barnacles, and in some areas carry a thick coiffure of glossy Rockweed, cover for a variety of small creepy-crawlies, as well as a multitude of common sea-mussels and *Littorines* ("periwinkles").

This morning I succumbed to a schoolboy urge to turn over a likely-looking rock and disturbed a busily-scuttling conclave of small Purple Shore-crabs, including a number of juveniles with the strange white patterns on their little carapaces (*Plate 25*). Feeling like an unwelcome intruder, I carefully lowered the heavy rock back into its

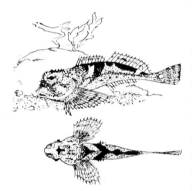

original place, hoping I had caused no lasting distress to anyone down there.

Occasionally too, I find undamaged shells of butter clams, scallops, limpets, dog whelks, and other small denizens of the sea, and can never resist putting these in my pocket, so as to bring them home and draw the intriguing geometrical shapes of these lovely little organisms. As I write, the shelf above my drawing table is lined with this biological bric-a-brac.

As I sat, soaking up the hot sunshine on a big log of driftwood, my friend the Great Blue Heron came, lazily flapping along the shore, and put down his long slender legs into a shallow pool of seawater twenty yards or so in front of me. He had apparently not observed me, sitting stock still among the great driftwood logs, for he took no notice of my presence, though he was unusually close to me, and herons are generally very shy, wary birds. As I watched, he began to walk very slowly and carefully forward in his pool, lifting one leg very gently out of the water, and setting it down again a few inches forward without making the slightest ripple in the surface of the water such as might alert the small sculpins and other tiny creatures to his presence and send them scuttling under the stones for cover. Evidently, though, this morning's pickings in this particular pool were disappointing. Not once did I witness one of those unerring, lightning-swift thrusts of the needle-sharp bill which normally mark the nemesis of some wriggling morsel of living prey, and in a very few minutes the big bird once again got up in that leisurely-seeming manner and flapped off down the shore in search of better fishing. I watched his progress until he again set himself down among the clamourous assemblage of seagulls and crows which are always present at the place where Cypress Creek empties itself into the sea.

The line of driftwood logs on which I so often sit and sun myself for a few moments on my morning walks forms an interesting and ever-changing pattern which might present a worthy challenge to an artist's pencil. Some of the larger logs, butt-ends of tree trunks four or five feet in diameter, appear to be permanently imbedded in the sand; but each occurrence of an extra high tide re-floats most of the logs and rearranges them in different positions, as well as — usually — adding some newcomers to the collection. There is also an ever-changing assortment of "dunnage," pieces of more-or-less waterlogged saw lumber, some of which can be "beach-combed," dried, and put to useful purposes, provided it does not carry a brand mark showing a rightful owner's name. My neighbour, friend, and erstwhile colleague, Gordon Tallman, has an eagle eye for prize

HEART COCKLE
Clinocardium nuttallii

KEYHOLE LIMPET
Diodora aspera

CHANNELED WHELK
Thais canaliculata

EDIBLE BLUE MUSSEL
Mytilus edulis

BUTTER CLAM
Saxidomus giganteus

BULL KELP
Nereocystus leutkeana

ROCK WEED
Fucus sp.

PLATE XXV

pieces of such jetsam, and seems able to spot choice bits of oak, mahogany, cherry, and other good hardwoods, upon which he exercises his very considerable craftsmanship to fashion beautiful objects of household usefulness. My own "finds" seem to consist only of worse-for-wear planks of fir or cedar, suitable only for the most plebeian of uses!

July 5   July is the butterfly month. Dr. W.J. Holland, of the *Butterfly Book* fame, called it the "gala time of the butterflies," and in those areas where flowery meadows are commonplace, this is very manifestly the case. But the common habitat presented by this mountainous coast is one of sombre forests, relatively poor in species of broad-leaved trees which in other areas form the food-plants for the caterpillars of many butterfly species, and only the flower-gardens of the local residents provide the bright sunny spaces where butterflies love to congregate. Nevertheless, many fine species do brighten our roadsides during this normally warmest of the summer months. This morning, many of the big yellow Swallowtails are to be seen soaring high over the housetops, or dropping down to sip at *Philadelphus* or other sweet-scented blossoms.

A common flowering shrub in our local gardens is the Buddleia, sometimes called the "Butterfly Bush" because of the strong attraction to these insects presented by its long, dense racemes of fragrant lavender-coloured blossoms. The Buddleia, though not a native, is evidently well suited to this particular area, for it readily escapes the confines of gardens in which it has been planted, and is to be seen in the roadside ditches and in many waste spaces along the route of my morning walks. On most warm, sunny July mornings, including this morning, I approach one especially dense thicket of the fragrant plant, hoping to be rewarded by the sight of a group of "Painted Lady" butterflies, one of the best known and most universally distributed of all the butterfly tribe, and known to love the Buddleia plant (*Plate 26*). On one such morning, two or three years ago, I was enthralled to see this particular bush all a-flutter with a dozen or more of the beautiful insects, their tawny wings catching the morning sunshine as they busily imbibed the heady nectar. Each July, when the Buddleia is at its best, I hope to be witness to a repeat performance, but so far it has not happened. The reason is not far to seek. The Painted Lady is a celebrated migrant, and for reasons not yet understood, travels in enormous swarms from one area to another, and it is only when individuals from such a swarm manage to reach the coast that we are rewarded with their

presence in our gardens. On one occasion, travelling southward by car down the Okanagan Valley from Salmon Arm to Princeton, BC, we found ourselves driving through clouds of butterflies, thousands upon thousands of Painted Ladies, all flying resolutely south-westwards, across our path. I think, though my diary does not clearly reveal it, that this must have been the same year in which I later witnessed the wonderful display on the Buddleia bush during my morning foray. But this morning, though the sun was shining bright and warm, and the Buddleia alive with bees, wasps, and hover-flies, not a Painted Lady was to be seen.

The common thistle (*carduus*) which forms the food-plant for the Painted Lady caterpillars, and from which the insect's scientific name, *Cynthia cardui*, is derived, is a fairly plentiful weed in our local waste areas, and when another swarm of the elusive Ladies does appear, there will doubtless be many excellent opportunities to observe and study its interesting early stages.

The residue of yellow-jacket wasps which survived my clumsy and *July 10* inexpert effort to destroy the colony, has given up its attempt to rebuild the city. They have laid down a flat but thickish mat of paper layers along one side of the house beam, evidently driven by a blind urge to cover up that which had been improperly exposed. They have built no new cells, and presumably that group of wasps programmed to build egg cells did not survive my holocaust, only the roofers, not the interior construction workers; for it is known that among these highly-developed "social" insects – wasps as well as bees and ants – groups or castes of the insects are specialized to carry out certain tasks in the work of the colony. But all activity in this fruitless effort along the roof beam has now ceased, and it is altogether probable that the wasps are now all dead, for it is the opinion of many entomological scholars, those who make a special study of the "social" insects, that the worker wasps do, in fact, die of exhaustion, literally working themselves to death.

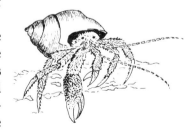

My route this morning was once again along the beach, with the sea at low half-tide and calm, and the sky partly overcast with the suggestion of a summer shower to come. I was unable to cross Cypress Creek where it runs out across the beach, for the flow is still strong, and the boulders too far-spaced to be reliable as stepping-stones. There are, no doubt, still pockets of snow high up on the mountain side, feeding the creek with their melt, and it is always late in the season before the creek is shrunken sufficiently to permit a safe and dry crossing on stones and drift-logs. I therefore picked

PAINTED LADY or
THISTLE BUTTERFLY
Cynthia cardui

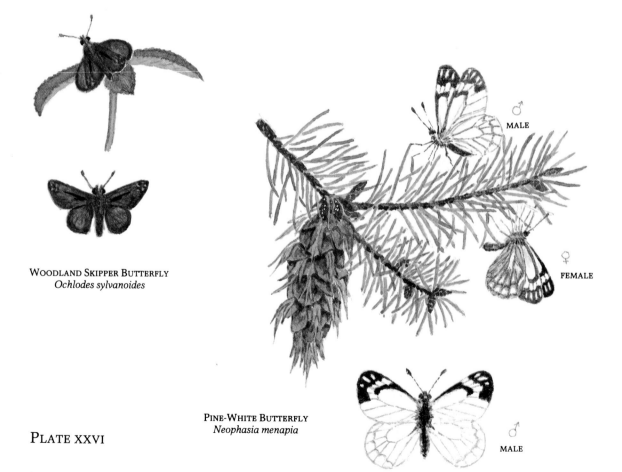

WOODLAND SKIPPER BUTTERFLY
Ochlodes sylvanoides

♂ MALE

♀ FEMALE

PINE-WHITE BUTTERFLY
Neophasia menapia

♂ MALE

PLATE XXVI

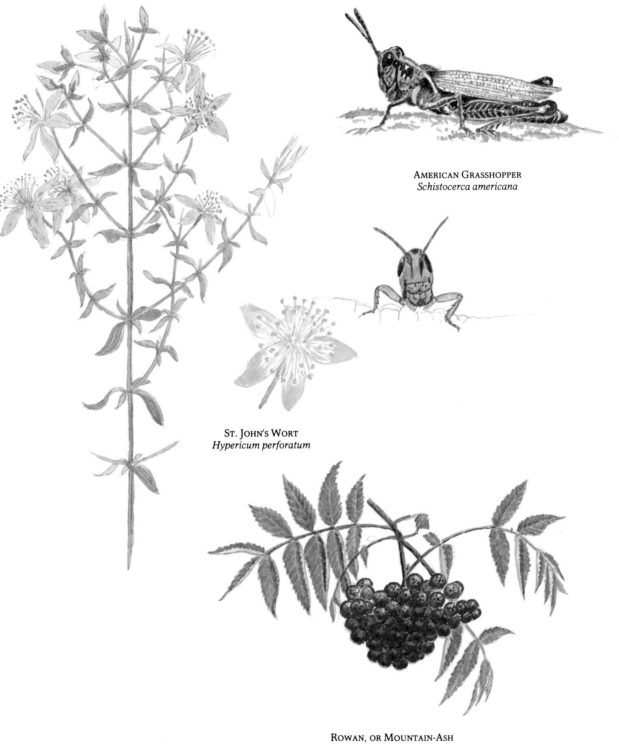

AMERICAN GRASSHOPPER
Schistocerca americana

ST. JOHN'S WORT
Hypericum perforatum

ROWAN, OR MOUNTAIN-ASH
Sorbus sitchensis

PLATE XXVII

my way along the boulders on the near bank of the stream, as I usually do, to cross by means of the bridge at Marine Drive. But today I sat for a short space on a clean, smooth rock, enjoying the babble of the creek, the gentle splashing of the small breaking waves along the shore, and the distant clamour of the gulls and crows at the surf-line. As I sat, a Belted Kingfisher came flying low along the creek-side, a streak of slate-gray, black and white, and with a sharp call came to rest on an overhanging branch a little distance downstream from me, where he sat with a beady eye intent on the prospect of a small unwary fish in the rockpools below him.

I was about to rise and continue my walk, when I noticed, to my surprise, far upstream and in the exact middle of the flowing creek, a young deer, a doe, walking in an apparently leisurely manner toward me. I froze into complete immobility, to watch what would happen. Evidently completely unaware of my presence, the beautiful, graceful creature continued toward me, keeping strictly in the centre of the stream, no doubt an instinctive act of caution usual to the species, and passed within ten feet of me, on her way toward the sea. She was astonishingly sure-footed on the slippery stones and rushing water as she continued right down the middle of the stream to its point of entry into the surf. The company of crows and gulls took not the slightest notice of her as she, finding no more creek to walk in, moved over on to the wet sand and back up the beach some yards behind me, then up onto the lawn of one of the waterside residences and into their shrubbery where she vanished from my view.

It is not at all unusual for these Black-tailed Coast Deer to find their way down from the mountainside forest into our populated area. The mountain streams, flowing in deep gullies, give the animals an opportunity to do so without their having to cross two busy and frightening highways. It is always a delight to obtain such a close, clear view of the deer, which quite commonly appear in people's gardens. But to some, not an entirely unmitigated delight, for the deer have a reprehensible appetite for tulip and hyacinth bulbs and other horticultural treasures, and maledictions are frequently called down on them by irate gardeners in the vicinity.

July 15   The advancing season produces its mutations and changes as the year wears on. The differences are imperceptible from one day to the next, but become noticeable as I pass some particular shrub or plant on two occasions a week or so apart. The tender yellowish-green of the spring leaves in May gives place to the deep rich green of the full summer. The landscape takes on a dryer appearance, even in this relatively moist coastal area, the grasses full-seeded and in some cases, brown and sere. The blackberry brambles this particular July are heavily loaded with fruit, but so far the berries, myriad in number, are still green, or only slightly tinted with red. Another two or three weeks of warm sunshine will produce a magnificent crop of the luscious black fruit.

The insects of late summer, too, are beginning to appear, and as I stride along my uphill route, I am continually starting up the large grasshoppers which are especially plentiful in this rocky terrain. With their long straight forewings closed together over their backs, they remain virtually invisible as they sit motionless upon the ground, for they are a marvel of camouflage, and are capable of adjusting their coloration to suit the background against which they rest (*Plate 27*). But upon my close approach the great powerful back legs, tensed like a catapult, kick out straight and fling the creature high into the air, where the four outspread wings take over, the broad hinder pair spread like a fan, border-patterned in lemon-yellow and black, and the grasshopper, with a dry, rasping "click-click-click" flies rapidly away for a few yards, only to settle down again, close its wings and disappear utterly from view. The grasshoppers are voracious vegetarians, and their number, during late July and August, is great. But they do not appear, in this coastal area, to inflict serious damage, unlike the somewhat smaller, but infinitely more numerous, grasshoppers of the prairie provinces, or the very much larger and still more numerous migratory grasshoppers (locusts) of the African continent. If I were so unfortunate as to become lost in our Canadian wilderness, I hope I should remember that grasshoppers are readily edible, with a texture, it is said, not unlike that of shrimp. The natives of certain African tribes do, certainly, eat the bodies of the migratory locusts, and the good St. John the Baptist is scripturally reported to have done so too, though he, it is written, varied the diet with "wild honey"—a somewhat difficult and hazardous comestible to obtain, one would imagine, in its raw wilderness state!

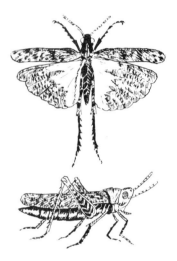

I noticed also today, that the "skipper" butterflies are beginning to make their appearance. These tiny members of the lepidopterous order are considered by some scientific authors to represent a sub-order intermediate between the butterflies and the moths, based on a number of taxonomic details which have no place in this Diary of a Quiet Pedestrian, who will continue to regard them as a family of true butterflies. Due to their small size and the rapid darting zig-zag flight which earns them their name of "skippers," they are sometimes exceedingly difficult to follow with the eye, especially on a very warm day, when they are most active and their insect metabolism at its most rapid. But they can be watched at quite close quarters as they feed, greedily, on the sweet-scented flowers of late summer. Today I observed a number of them, (Woodland Skippers – *Ochlodes sylvanoides* – which is the common species hereabouts) thrusting their long prosbosces into the central florets of some single Dahlia blossoms, and noted particularly the peculiar resting position of the Skipper tribe, the forewings held butterfly-fashion vertically over the back, and the hinder pair spread out moth-like on either side of the body. These strange little insects, ruddy-brown in colour, feed as caterpillars on various grasses, and the skippers themselves can sometimes be seen in swarms in grassy fields. They will increase in numbers as the late summer wears on, and will be around, no doubt, when all other butterflies have vanished.

July 20    The Pine White butterflies (*Neophasia menapia*) which I usually associate with the month of August, have begun to show up (*Plate 26*), and I am wondering whether their early appearance will signal a serious infestation of these insects on our fine Douglas Fir trees. Today, as I start out, I noticed two or three of the male butterflies fluttering about the tops of two exceptionally tall firs growing across the street from my house. The Cabbage Whites are still about in numbers, as they continue to be throughout the summer, and when, some years ago I first encountered the Pine White, I thought I was looking at a somewhat tired specimen of the Cabbage White! But this "tired" appearance is, as they say, "diagnostic," for the Pine White is an exceedingly delicate little insect, and although it is of about the same size as the Cabbage White, and has the same general coloration, white with black markings, the pattern of markings is entirely different, and its flight is slow and feeble-looking, in strong contrast to the vigorous, rapid progress of the Cabbage butterfly. The weak fluttering flight is a sure identifying mark of the Pine White species.

I have no doubt that, as the month of August approaches, the tops of the neighbouring fir trees will be all a-flutter with the little white dancers, the males of the species. A little later on, the females will appear around the lower branches of the trees. These have a more yellowish appearance in flight, for, though the upper surfaces of the wings are pure white, like those of the males, the undersides of the hind-wings exhibit a strong pattern of heavy gray veins with saffron-yellow margins, giving the yellowish appearance when the females are in flight. During the morning hours the males descend

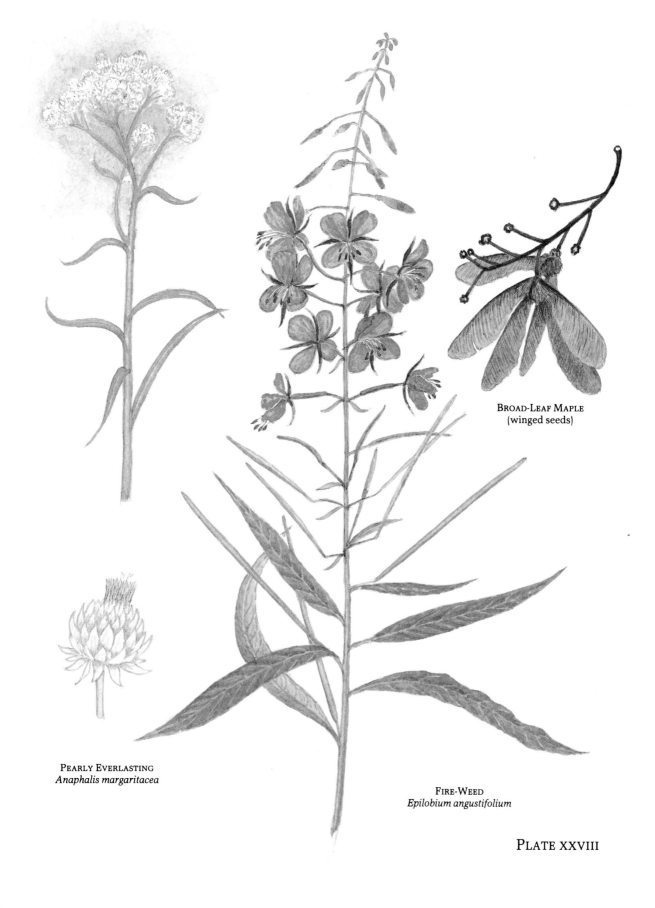

PEARLY EVERLASTING
Anaphalis margaritacea

BROAD-LEAF MAPLE
(winged seeds)

FIRE-WEED
Epilobium angustifolium

PLATE XXVIII

from their high-flying and mate with the females, which then deposit their eggs at the base of the fir needles. This can be a serious matter, for the resulting caterpillars can, in some years, make serious depredations on the fir trees, to the concern of tree-lovers in our area. Fortunately, the insects appear to occur only in three to four-year cycles. Last year and the year before there were few if any Pine White butterflies in this area, but I fear there may well be a serious infestation this year.

July 25 The roadside ditches and verges, too, alter their appearance as the weeks go by. The yellow buttercups and the lawn dandelions are mostly gone, and are replaced by a variety of later weeds, including a number of species of plants of the composite order, bearing small yellow dandelion-like flowers which seed themselves in the form of small round dandelion "clocks," numerous on the tops of long branching stems. I have not, so far, been able to sort these out as to exact species, and I am assured by my botanist friends that to do so accurately is a difficult and puzzling job.

The St. John's Wort is still brightening the roadsides with dense heads of golden-yellow stars, and the "Pearly Everlasting" is just opening its flat panicles of blossom (*Plate 28*). This late-blooming member of the composite order is extremely interesting, and the tight spherical buds, which do indeed resemble pearls, are worth a close examination under a good magnifying glass, revealing unexpected beauty. The wooly undersurfaces of the leaves, and the fact that the spent flowers do not wither but persist well into the winter months, make the Pearly Everlasting a favourite for winter indoor decoration.

The broad area skirting the north side of McKechnie Park where, in the springtime, I observed and reported upon the feathery growth of the Mares-tail plant, is now richly overgrown with the Asiatic (or Himalayan) Snapweed, a tall and very decorative *Impatiens*, which at some period was brought into this area as a garden perennial but has escaped and spread itself luxuriantly over roadside ditches, railway embankments, and waste spaces everywhere. The flowers, numerous on the three-foot-high plants, vary in colour from palest shell-pink to rose-purple, and are of a strange design, somewhat resembling the totally unrelated Snapdragon. It is amusing to watch the bees finding their way into these blossoms, alighting on the broad "lip," which obligingly drops down a little under the bee's feather weight, inviting it to enter. The bee does so, and the lip thereupon closes, completely hiding the insect's activities within. In order to observe and record these, I once spent an entertaining and instructive few hours making close-range motion-pictures of the operation, to do which I cut, with a scalpel, a neat window in the side of one of the flowers, and was indeed able to obtain a good pictorial record of the bee probing with its long tongue into the nectary of the flower. The unexpected opening, however, completely confused the bee, which came out through it instead of backing out of the flower in the normal way, and re-entered the same flower via the lip, and out again at the artificial window, several times before overcoming its apparent bewilderment. The showing of this film-sequence never fails to produce hilarity.

Today I noticed that, standing well up above these Snapweeds were several handsome spires of Fireweed (*epilobium*) in full bloom with its rich pink four-petalled flowers. It is obviously a potassium-loving plant, for it is known to be about the first to appear in forest-areas laid waste by forest fire, hence its popular North American name, Fireweed. As a boy in England I knew this same plant by the name "Rosebay Willow-herb," a common and beautiful wildflower which grew plentifully along the willow-lined banks of the Wey River and the Basingstoke Canal, close to my boyhood home at Weybridge, in the county of Surrey. But in London, during the Second World War, among the charred and blackened debris of the "Blitz," there very soon began to appear patches of this same graceful plant, its wind-carried seeds having doubtless been blown in from adjacent country areas and nourished by the potash leached out from the ashes of the burned-out city. It is now, not surprisingly, also called Fireweed in Britain.

Our large, highly-polished picture windows have, alas, claimed *July 27* another casualty, this time a diminutive Golden-Crowned Kinglet, next to the hummingbird, our smallest native bird. We usually see small flights of these feathered mites going through on the spring and autumn migrations, but this seems a little early for the southward flight to have commenced. It seems to be during these migratory flights, with their somewhat headlong nature, that birds are most prone to injure or kill themselves in this manner.

I brought the pathetic little carcass into the house to make a drawing and to wonder anew at the perfection of the minute flight-feathers, the incredible softness of the downy back and rump, the brilliance of the yellow poll, the delicacy of the tiny clawed feet.

Sudden death, even in a tiny bird, never fails to awake in me a feeling of regret, and, in this case something also of guilt, and I find myself hoping that the mite felt nothing; just as, when I read of a tragic airplane disaster, I pray that, for those who perished, it was quick!

August

August 4   The sixty-seventh anniversary of the outbreak of the war which was "to *end* war" but which did nothing to end war, but only sowed the seeds of further and equally terrible conflicts, yet changed the lives of everyone for all time. To most people nowadays, except for us oldsters, August 4th, 1914 means little, for the veterans of that First World War are almost gone, and those even of the 1939-45 conflict are now becoming middle-aged or elderly men and women in an altered world. To me, a youngster not yet thirteen, just entering four years of secondary school, the tumult and the shouting, the alarums and excursions of August 1914 were exciting times, for to me and my companions, the terrors of those dreadful four years had not yet come home.

This morning, as I made my way up this lovely hillside, and looked out over the peaceful scene of prosperous homes and well-tended gardens, I was moved to wonder what the future holds in store for other thirteen-year-olds, including my own grandchildren, one of whom, a healthy redhead, will be thirteen this fall. For the clouds on the political horizon, like those which are filling our sky this morning, are ominous. But these gloomy musings are, after all, not natural history, and there is, as always, much around me to take my mind off the world's many troubles.

August might well be characterized the Month of Fruiting, for many of the trees and shrubs which delighted the eye, and the nostril, in May and early June with drifts of heavy-scented blossom, are now loaded with handsome and sometimes brightly-coloured fruit. The Mountain Ash, which Scottish folk know by the more attractive name of Rowan, is especially prolific in berries this year. Some of the trees I have passed today have their masses of berries a strong deep orange in colour, while on others the fruit is true clear vermilion red (*Plate 29*). As far as I know, there are not two separate species, or varieties of the Rowan tree to account for this colour-variation, and I can only assume that local variations in soil chemistry are what give rise to the phenomenon.

The Mountain Ash must surely be one of the hardiest, and most tenacious of life, of all our native trees, seeming to thrive in the most

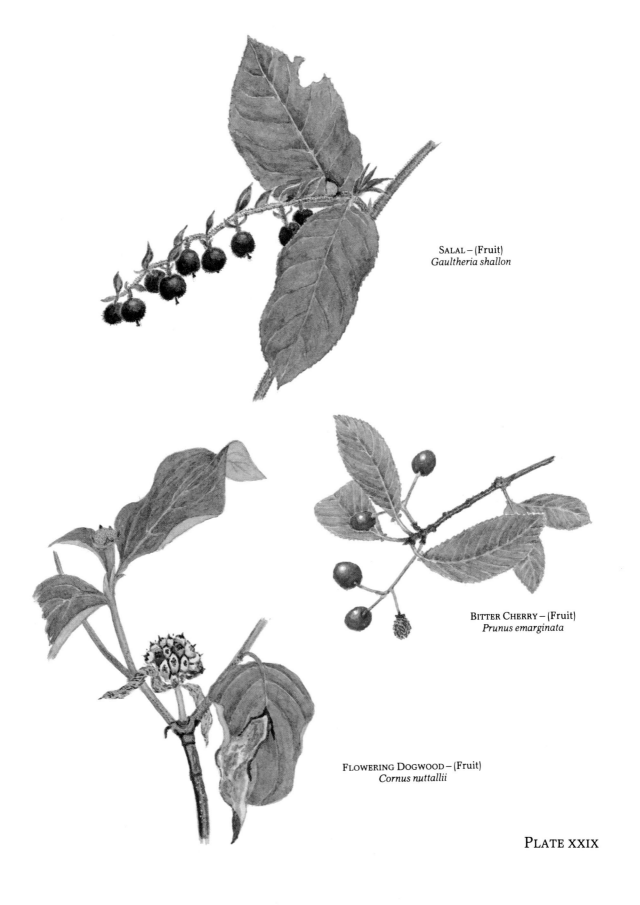

SALAL – (Fruit)
Gaultheria shallon

BITTER CHERRY – (Fruit)
Prunus emarginata

FLOWERING DOGWOOD – (Fruit)
Cornus nuttallii

PLATE XXIX

unlikely places. We have two in our garden, both of them "sports," i.e. not intentionally planted, one of these, particularly, being in a place where we do not want it. But it stubbornly resists all efforts to eradicate it. Three times now, we have cut its multiple stems clean back to the roots, but each ensuing spring it sends up a new crop of healthy shoots, and the following summer there are flowers, with berries to follow. Today, the second August after such a drastic cutback, it is again a mass of vermilion fruit, which will delight the southward-hastening birds in the coming months. We cannot uproot the obstinate tree, for it is growing on a bare rock slope, and appears to spring out of the solid granite! One tends to think of the Rowan as a shrub or a very small tree. But each morning my route takes me past a noble one, with a foot-diameter trunk, at the present moment aflame with a mass of the bright berries. Growing as one of a pair with an equally stately Locust, or Acacia tree, it lends dignity to the small wooden house and charming English-style garden in which it stands.

The Bitter Cherry, one of the commonest and least valued of our "weed trees" is also now in fruit. The bunches of rather insignificant white five-petalled flowers were in bloom in May and were heavily relied upon by early bees and other spring insects. The small glossy red cherries, each on its half-inch stalk, are now fully ripe and, like the Rowan-berries, much favoured by fruit-eating birds. I do not know whether the taste buds of birds bear any similarity to the well-developed ones of the human species, but these small wild cherries are, to us, extremely bitter to the taste. The Bitter Cherry is quite often referred to as the "Pin Cherry," but this last-named is actually a separate, though closely-related species found only east of the Rocky Mountain Divide. The Bitter Cherry is the only species of wild cherry found in this coastal area.

August 10   The Salal bushes in McKechnie Park, which in June were displaying long graceful stems of pale-pink blossoms, each a small inverted bell, as in the flowers of most members of the great Heather family, are now heavy with big circular black berries, which, to me, taste not unlike an unripe gooseberry. The Coast Indians are said to make some kind of medicinal decoction of these berries, but what therapeutic qualities are claimed for it I have no idea. In spite of the present profusion of the Salal berries, I do not find myself at all tempted to eat them as I take my morning walks.

This, however, I cannot claim with reference to the Blackberries, which now are at their ripest and best, hanging in heavy black masses on the dense bramble thickets at several points along my route up the mountainside, and the time taken for my peregrination, normally just an hour for the three-mile circuit, is always substantially longer during the blackberry harvest, for then I make rather more frequent pauses to study nature (*Plate 30*). And eat blackberries. Sometimes too – this morning, for example – I carry some kind of container with me and bring home a litre or so of the luscious fruit upon which my Constant Companion may exercise her not-inconsiderable culinary skill. Jam, jelly, hopefully, a pie!

The Flowering Dogwood is now, also, in the fruiting stage, and the rough hemispherical clusters, usually in the center of a circlet of leaves, are already breaking down into a multitude of the angular-shaped seeds.

The tall spires of Fireweed are now fully seeded. The handsome   *August 14* rose-pink flowers are practically all finished, and the long rod-like seed-capsules have split along their length and curled back, each releasing a myriad of minute seeds, each on its own tiny white parachute. As a result the flower heads are now a downy mass of the silvery material, and at every gentle puff of wind a host of the little parachutes detach themselves and go floating away, seeking fresh pastures.

I never fail to be amazed at the utter profligacy displayed by nature in arranging that living organisms – the Fireweed plant is an excellent example – develop and disperse uncountable numbers of embryonic offspring, in order to ensure that some few will survive. For only some few are intended to survive, and on those occasions when the delicate balance is disturbed, or the natural controls of one species or another are not sufficiently present, we are faced with a superabundance of that particular species, a swarm, a plethora, an infestation, depending on how welcome or unwelcome the superabundance may be.

Similarly, the Himalayan Snapweed surrounding the Fireweed plants in a dense growth along the border of McKechnie Park has now developed and ripened its explosive seed pods, and I have only to thrust my hand into a group of the plant tops, and a dozen or more of the ripe capsules will split with an almost audible "click," their several sections springing back into a tight coil, and throwing the large black seeds, ten to a pod, far and wide over a considerable area. Surely, one has only to contemplate the dimensions of this mighty struggle among the natural species, both animal and vegetable, each to maintain its identity and continuity in competi-

RED ALDER (female seed cones)
Alnus rubra

TRAILING BLACKBERRY
Rubus ursinus

KNOTWEED (OR "BISTORT")
Polygonum aviculare

PLATE XXX

tion with all comers, to recognize the extreme delicacy of the system that holds it all in equilibrium in "the Balance of Nature," and to admonish ourselves that we disturb it at our peril.

This appears to be wedding season for the Ants, of which there are, naturally, many species in this generally wooded area. This morning, as I sat for a few moments on a fallen log at one of my customary resting places, a number of what people often describe to me as "flying ants" came to my notice. These were a very small species of ant, and they were crawling up out of a fissure in the surface of the log, their gossamer wings gleaming faintly in the morning sun. Each one would pause a moment, then spread its delicate wings and take off into the air for the nuptial or mating flight common to all ant species. For the ants, like many species of wasps and bees, are social insects, and in the complicated social structure of the ant colony, most of the ants are either "workers" or "soldiers" – in both cases sexless females with certain closely-defined duties to perform within the nest. But some, by means of special feeding, are, as with the bees and wasps, developed into fully-sexed males and females, and as soon as these emerge from the cocoons the workers attend and curry them, and the soldiers drive them out of the nest, to fly off and consummate their mating on the wing. Which being accomplished they fly or fall back to earth, the males die, and the fertilized females bite off their own or each others' wings and crawl away to find a location for the start of a new colony.

This morning I examined the ground for some distance around me, and did, sure enough, find one or two of the minute creatures engaged in the contortion which seems to accompany the act of getting rid of their now useless wings. But because of their very small size it was somewhat difficult to examine them in close detail. Some years ago, however, I had reason to remove a large flat stone which was lying in a waste area, and uncovered a large company of the big, and much more easily visible, black ants, the males and females with their long transparent wings being groomed and prepared by a vast and active assemblage of ant-world bridesmaids, and was able to secure some first-rate motion picture footage of the busy scene before, in common decency, replacing the stone.

The birds are beginning to congregate in and around the local gardens, no doubt in early preparation for the southward migration. The great trek is not yet "on," but there is a significant increase in the number of birds one sees in flight and feeding among the bushes, compared to the earlier summer when many were busy about their mating and family-raising activities in the forest further north. But lines of swallows are beginning to appear on the telephone wires, and the resounding cheer of the Red-shafted Flicker, that most attractive of woodpeckers, seldom heard during the mating season, is now much in evidence among the tall firs and cedars.

I must now again lay in a stock of wild-bird seed for the feeder which hangs outside our kitchen window for the migrating swarms that will soon appear to entertain my Constant Companion as she goes about her daily tasks. My ornithological friends tell me that it is not good to feed the birds too lavishly, if at all, during the birds' family-raising period, when, in any case, natural food is readily available, and when the newly-arrived young birds thrive best on the natural "mix" of foods brought to them by their parents. But during the height of the migrations, the birds can well accept all the rich nourishment they can get, in preparation for the rigours of the long journey. In his book *High Jungle* the late Dr. William Beebe, that greatest of naturalists, tells in his delightful prose of the manner in which some of the tiniest birds, such as warblers, stuff themselves with protein-rich food in preparation for the long northward flight from the jungled mountains of Venezuela to, in some cases, even as far as central Canada; this journey including a non-stop crossing of the Caribbean and the Gulf of Mexico. I trust that my prepared mix of millet, cracked corn, oats, wheat, and sunflower-seeds will help to sustain them on their southbound search for greener pastures. In any event, the Spotted Towhee, the Oregon Junco, the Black-capped Chickadee, the House Finch, the Evening Grosbeak, will all soon be back in numbers, quarrelsomely jostling each other on the feeder and spilling much of the grain on to the ground below.

August 25   The Steller's Jays are already here, very much and very noisily in evidence (*Plate 31*). Some of them are about the area throughout the year, although in their case too, their raucous clamour is noticeably less during the mating period than earlier and later in the year. For all their noise and all their greedy gobbling of food, they are a joy to behold with their gorgeous blue plumage, their black crested heads, and their even blacker beady, knowing eyes. And they are, withal, the most hilarious of avian comics, purveyors of endless amusement if one is able to tolerate their bullying behaviour towards other, less aggressive birds, and does not attempt to apply human morals to their avian antics.

They become extremely tame, confiding, and even bold, once they become convinced that I bear them no ill-will. And they have an insatiable appetite for peanuts. It is my custom, perhaps not unbecoming in an elderly citizen, to recline for half an hour or so after luncheon, on a chaise-lounge upon our sunny patio, when the weather is suitable for such outdoor dalliance. I take care to have peanuts secreted in my shirt or trousers pocket, and I have usually not stretched myself out more than a minute or two before the blue panhandlers arrive with a raucous cheer, looking for the expected handout. They take the first two or three nuts directly from my hand, the sharp black claws taking a momentary grip around one of my fingers as the bird seizes the peanut, then flies off to the stone parapet of the patio, or to the edge of one of our planter tubs, where it grips the peanut firmly between its two feet and breaks open the shell with strong blows of its sharp black bill. The jays then give me no peace until all peanuts are delivered – and for some time after all are gone and they are finally convinced of the fact. They fly all around me, perching on everything as close as possible to where I lie; and in final desperation they perch on my outstretched shoe, hop along my legs and body, and even poke their cheeky heads into my pockets in search of the further provender they feel certain must still be there. Until finally, with a squawk of seeming derision, they make off in evident disgust.

Each spring, for the past two or three years, a pair of these birds has arrived, one of them – I believe the male – being bolder and tamer than the other, and always the first to feed from my hand. Then for some weeks they disappear, only to return in August with two or more others in attendance, and I have been inclined to assume, though with not much hard evidence, that these are "children" hatched and raised during the period of absence. But these children, if that is indeed what they are, have now gone their way and the original pair, now well recognizable to us, are back at their antics. But there are many of the jays about, and as I went my way this morning, many a flash of blue feathers passed before me from one tall tree to another, and many an avian Bronx cheer from among the green foliage.

All the jay tribe seem to be endowed with the same aggressive, bold, mischievous habits. The Eastern Blue Jay, very similar to our Steller's Jay except for its blue, white, and black coloration, is known to behave in the same manner, and I was surprised, some years ago in the jungle-clad mountains of Venezuela, to see flocks of the Green

GOLDEN-CROWNED KINGLET
Regulus satrapa
Killed by impact with picture-window

BELTED KINGFISHER
Megaceryle alcyon

STELLER'S JAY
Cyanocitta stelleri

PLATE XXXI

Jay, again exactly alike in form, size, and habits, differing only in its green, yellow, and black plumage from the Blue and the Steller's Jays of our Canadian woods. The Gray Jay, or "Whiskey Jack," is quite a common bird in the forest a little higher up our mountainside, but I have not seen them in the lower, populated area about which I walk and write. The Gray Jay does not seem to have the raucous call of the Blue and the Steller's—in fact I have found it to be very quiet in the woods. But the lumbermen's nickname for it, "camp robber," speaks for itself!

September

September 1   After a day or so of cooler weather with some rain and wind, September is today ushered in with a return of bright sunshine and warmth. Last night the almost-full moon cast a path of silver across the bay, on a sea of glassy stillness and calm. But there is a hint of autumn in the air. Although the wayside is still generally green and glossy, here and there a Broad-leaved Maple shows a branch, or perhaps just a few leaves prematurely bright golden yellow, foretaste of the glory that is to come. The dogwoods, too, their seeds now almost all dispersed, are beginning to shed their foliage, and some of the fallen leaves display bizarre patterns of deep red, yellow, and green.

The ravens this morning are very busy. The tall hemlocks in McKechnie Park are full of their croaking call, the deep notes of the mature birds and the lighter, not-quite-perfect efforts of what are evidently the newly-arrived juveniles.

The Pine-white butterflies have now largely disappeared, no doubt discouraged by the recent cool wet days, and it is evident the infestation of these insects that I feared has not materialized. There were in fact few females among them this year, so possibly no serious damage will have been inflicted on next season's growth.

September 7   Labour Day – a public holiday dedicated to the dignity of labour, about which pious utterances continue to be made from pulpit and rostrum while upon the actual labour scene dignity seems currently to have been forgotten. Few seem to have heard of John Ruskin, but the Apostles of Profit and the Apostles of Wages face one another in ever more stubborn confrontations. Meanwhile productivity suffers, the conversion of natural resources into wealth goes by default, the world's work remains undone and the economy falters and seems likely to grind to a standstill. It may perhaps be a sort of escapism, but there is a measure of comfort to be derived from a contemplation of the web of life which binds together the miniature world of the undergrowth among the thickets of the roadside wastes, as I pause for a brief rest on my daily journey. Confrontations there are, to be sure, sometimes savage ones of life and death, but never of evil ill-will, and always one has a wondrous sense of the balance and harmony which hold it all together.

Not far from where I stand there is a patch of wet mud along the edges of a puddle drying up after yesterday's heavy rain. On and around it, a number of Yellow-footed Mud-daubers are busily at work, digging furiously into the mud and flying off with a little ball of it gripped between front legs and jaws (*Plate 32*). These graceful long-legged, long-bodied wasps are members of a "solitary" group, not living in a complex social colony as in the case of the yellow-jacketed paper-wasps that have already made their debut elsewhere in these papers. The physical structure of these creatures never fails to amaze me, for the thorax and front part of the body are separated from the abdomen by a long "wasp-waist" of hair-like thinness. The head and thorax, as in all insects, contain all the organs of locomotion—the muscles that work the six legs and four wings, as well as the insect "heart," the sensory organs comprising the "brain," and the mouthparts for feeding the organism. But the abdomen, trailing far behind at the end of the long "waist," contains the digestive organs as well as those of reproduction, including the ovipositor in the case of the females. All communication between the two "halves," the control of several important bodily functions, must pass to and fro along that tiny tubular body-section. But the insect flies with great delicacy and grace, its six long yellow legs trailing below it as it goes. These wasps are accomplished masons, and use the little balls of mud to construct small masonry cells for the rearing of the wasp progeny. Each female wasp works on her own, and it requires many trips to and from the source of the mud to complete each cell, which may be a couple of inches long, with a cylindrical inner chamber about the size of a large lead-pencil. The mud is mixed with wasp saliva and the cell, when finished, is hard and strong like well-made concrete. As each cell is completed, the wasp goes off on a spider hunt, and stings each luckless spider as she catches it, enough to paralyze it, but not yet kill it. Each immobilized arachnid is brought back and shoved into the cell, until the latter is filled, with eight or ten spiders. The wasp then lays an egg on the body of the topmost spider, and flies off for some more mud with which to close the open end of the cell. Then off again for still more mud with which to start another cell, usually alongside, and attached to, the first. Her activities and her industry are unceasing. "Hours of work and overtime" do not constitute a clause in her union contract. She works like a Fury. And she does get things done! And, ah yes, the wasp egg. Secure in the warm darkness, it very quickly hatches into an active grub – mostly a pair of strong jaws on not much of a body – which at once falls to and commences a non-stop meal of spiders – whose bodies will not decompose and poison the grub, since they are not dead but merely paralyzed – until all are consumed, when the grub will change into a chrysalis, and subsequently into a full-fledged Mud-dauber with jaws strong enough to gnaw its way to freedom and wasp-hood through the concrete door of the cell. As to where these particular Mud-daubers I have been watching are building their cells I do not know, and it is no easy matter to follow them home to find out. But it is doubtless under the shaded lower surface of some overhanging rock ledge. I have often found the cells in such places, and frequently under the overhanging concrete windowsill of a brick or stone building.

September 9 Today the weather is dull and a little blustery, with more than a hint of autumn, and a chill east wind is producing a minor surf, with the incoming tide at about half flow. The ever-changing character of the beach has this morning enabled me to walk in relative comfort along a strip of firm sand where on many another occasion I must traverse a course of barnacle-crusted stones, uneasy and uncomfortable on the feet. It is difficult to understand fully the various combinations of surf, tide and currents which give rise to these changes and alterations in the character of the shore line, even between successive tides.

This morning I found the flow in Cypress Creek so much reduced that I was able, for the first time in months, to cross on a series of stepping stones evidently put in place by the local children. This beach is a heaven-sent playground for youngsters with imagination, for the wealth of great hollow tree trunks, stranded logs, and bits and ends of timber of all shapes and sizes are an open invitation to small buccaneers to set up house and plan their dastardly doings. But today the pirate dens and the driftwood shacks and hidey-holes are deserted and forlorn, for Labour Day is past, the outlaws are back at school and the Three Rs hold sway. My thoughts went back seven decades to my own early boyhood with the reflection that things do not greatly change. To be sure, we did not have a broad sea beach, with the stranded trunks of great forest trees. But we had the common, the "Old Gold Common," a great tract of gorse and heather-grown sand hills, with small willow and birch trees whose supple stems and branches could be pulled together to form a kraal, a tepee, a fort, to be held at all costs against the assegais of the Zulus, the battle axes of the Picts and Scots, the arrows of the marauding

"WOOLY-BEAR" CATERPILLAR
Isia isabella

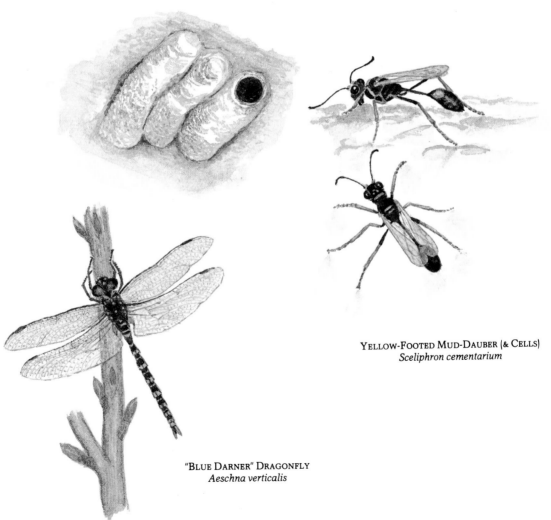

YELLOW-FOOTED MUD-DAUBER (& CELLS)
Sceliphron cementarium

"BLUE DARNER" DRAGONFLY
Aeschna verticalis

PLATE XXXII

Indians of the Plains, or whichever band of desperadoes we had most recently become acquainted with in our school reading. Then too, it all came to an abrupt end when the fell day rolled around for the return to school, the regret only partly tempered by the excitement of new readers, clean new exercise books, and fine new sharp pencils. Ah youth!

Having successfully negotiated the crossing, I sat for a time on a stranded stump in fairly close proximity to the hundred or so gulls which, as always, were holding their convention at the shoreline outflow of the creek. While most remain more or less stationary on the sand, watching for morsels of food brought down on the stream, there are always some of them coming and going in short wheeling flights, and their graceful aerobatics constitute a continuous ballet which it is a delight to watch. Always, they come in upwind in a smooth shallow glide to the point on which they intend to put down. Then with a slight upturn of the outstretched wings, a fanning-out of the tail feathers and a spread of the webbed feet, acting as air brakes, they come to a momentary and perfect standstill in the air exactly the right height above the sand to enable them to set their odd spindly legs gently down into the standing position – no staggering fluttering or wobbling, but a perfect two-point landing. Then they briefly fidget their long wings together neatly into position over their backs, not unlike a Victorian gentleman adjusting his coat tails when taking his seat in the drawing room. Taking off again, they spread the great wings, tilt them slightly upwards and allow the breeze to lift them gently a foot or so off the sand before they commence the powerful flapping that gets them on their way.

The whole manoeuvre illustrates in a very graphic way the principle of the "power glide" upon which modern aviation is based, though the "power" in the case of the sea gulls is the force of gravity plus their forward momentum as they slide down the air. Past generations of "bird-men" seem to have been preoccupied, while struggling with the problems of human flight, with efforts to reproduce by mechanical means the flapping wing of a bird, a well-nigh impossible project in view of the extreme complexity of the wing structure and its covering of feathers. Even the incomparable Leonardo da Vinci seems to have been unable to get his great mind beyond this view of the problem. It was not until the idea of the power glide came into the scientific mind, the power being supplied by a separate engine and propeller, that the age-old picture of aerial travel for mankind began at last to come into focus. It remained only for the clever and doggedly persevering Wright brothers to solve one of the principal remaining puzzles, that of lateral stability, by their invention of the dihedral angle between the wings, for aviation to get away to a "flying" start. These reflections cannot fail to exercise my mind – for I am an engineer – as I watch the lovely performance of these ever-present Glaucous-winged Gulls.

All are not equal, however, in their aerial prowess. For many of the gulls in the assemblage are juveniles, in various shades of gray plumage, from light-dappled to deep-dun, and it is very evident that some of these are still "just learning." The soft coloration of their babyhood, the exact hue of the granite rocks and a perfect camouflage and protection, changes noticeably each year for perhaps three, or even four years, before the gleaming white head and the soft blue-gray mantle are fully acquired, indicating maturity and mating, by which time they will long since have become the accomplished aeronauts I have attempted to portray.

September 16

The clear sunny September days have returned, a welcome extension to the summer. But as the equinox approaches, the sun each day is noticeably lower in the heavens, and the autumnal early-morning chill becomes increasingly evident, particularly in areas shaded by our big sombre conifers from the low morning sun. The sensation that fall is not far off is then very strong.

My attention was caught this morning by the bright colouring of a fairly large caterpillar, completely motionless on the hanging twig of an Ocean Spray shrub whose few remaining leaves have already turned a beautiful russet colour. The caterpillar, the larval form of the Isabella Tiger-moth, a common insect, was undoubtedly on its way to find a suitable cranny in which to spin up its neat oval cocoon for the winter sleep. But the night-time chill had evidently overtaken it and, it being a cold-blooded animal, its metabolism had slowed down to a point at which it was virtually immovable, as it lay along the leaf of the shrub, its orange mid-body and black furry front and rear ends plainly visible to the passerby. I continued on my way up the hillside, but, overcome with curiosity, slightly altered my normal circular route so as to re-pass the spot on my return to my house, thinking I might take the caterpillar home and make a drawing of it. By this time, however, the sun had lifted its limb sufficiently into the eastern sky to allow its morning rays to fall upon the little orange-and-black body, which had come to life, moved on, and was now nowhere to be seen. This inability of cold-blooded creatures to function actively in low temperatures must always have acted to some degree as a deterrent to the development of this particular form of life, and the subsequent emergence of warm-blooded forms like the mammals and birds must then, surely, have represented a vital "plateau" in the long uphill story of continuing creation.

This particular caterpillar is the one which, perhaps because of its peripatetic habit of busily scuttling about along the ground from one clump of plantain to the next, has endeared itself to generations of children who, in the English-speaking world, refer to it as the "wooly bear." French children, however, in days gone by, knew it as a "furry kitten"—"Chatte pelouse"—which, so we are told, is the origin of our word "caterpillar."

The late Dr. W.J. Holland, author of the famous *Butterfly Book* and the somewhat less well-known *Moth Book*, quotes one Topsell, writing in the year 1608 under the odd title *History of Serpents*, who had the following to say about these Arctiid caterpillars:

> There is another sort of these caterpillars, who haue no certain place of abode, nor yet cannot tell where te find theyr foode, but, like vnto superstitious Pilgrims, doo wander and stray hither and thither and....consume and eat up that which is none of theyr owne; and these haue purchased the very apt name among vs Englishmen, to be called Palmer-wormes, by reason of theyr wandering and rogish life (for they neuer stay in one place but are ever wandering) although by reason of theyr roughness and ruggedness, some doo call them "Beare-Wormes."

Wooly-bears, Furry-kittens, or Beare-wormes, their dense, bristly hair is an irritant to some skins, and in the days when I was actively engaged in collecting butterflies and moths for study, I forbore to handle these comical little creatures any more than necessary.

There are, indeed, many forms of insect life which for some reason seem to become more noticeable during the warm days of autumn, though many of them have without doubt been present all summer, perhaps less conspicuous among the burgeoning activities of so many wild forms during the crown of the year. The woods of McKechnie Park seem very silent, now that so many birds have taken their departure, and there is a certain feeling of sadness, as if so much of life were over and done. This of course is illusory, for the forces of rebirth are unceasing, and are already at work in seed-capsule, bulb, rootlet, larva, and cocoon. But many of the insects, while the weather stays warm, are still busily on the go.

A big handsome dragonfly has appeared, hawking back and forth

over the rock slope in our garden, a scourge to the less active flying insects on which it preys. I find myself wondering whence it came, for the early "nymph" stages of all dragonflies are spent in fresh water, where for two or three years they prey vigorously on the nymphs of the same hapless insects whose mature, flying stages engage the attention of the mature dragonflies. Our nearest fresh water is the nearby Cypress Creek, and I can only assume that some of the less turbulent pools along the course of that ofttimes raging little stream have provided homes and hunting grounds for the dragonfly nymphs. This big and very handsome fellow is a local representative of the *Aeschna* genus, commonly called the "Blue Darner." Dragonflies, especially in past times, have been the subject of much superstition and ignorant fear. During my early boyhood in the south of England, they were often known as "horse-stingers," perhaps because, apparently attracted to the salty warmth of a sweating horse, they were sometimes seen to settle on Dobbin's broad flank. But sting him they did not and could not, and they are completely harmless to everyone except the luckless prey-insects I have referred to. But I was surprised, when I first came to live in Canada as a very young man, to hear these insects referred to as "darning-needles," obviously because of the long slender body— needle-shaped, as it were. In any event, the name "darner" has persisted, and appears as the common name for dragonflies of this genus, even in some of the soberest of entomological texts.

Dragonflies, too, are superb aeronauts. They can show prodigious bursts of speed in the air, but can also hover completely motionless in one spot, or fly forwards, backwards, sideways or up and down with apparently equal ease. This aerial dexterity has been attributed by some authorities to the fact that dragonflies, unlike most other insects, can, and do, operate their four powerful wings independently of each other. Doubtless there is substance in this theory, but it is to be noted that the tiny Syrphid, or Hover Flies—somewhat resembling small wasps with their yellow and black striped bodies, are as good or even better aviators, and can hover motionless above the autumn flowers, or dart back and forward just as nimbly as the Blue Darner, yet have only two, not four wings on which to do so. For these are members of the *Diptera*, or Two-winged, order of insects, in which the forward pair of wings are used for flying, the hinder pair having, in the process of evolution, atrophied into tiny knobbed appendages called "halteres," whose continuing usefulness is not with certainty known, though several theories have been advanced.

I have noticed also, during the past warmish days, an unusually large number of the tiny, delicately-structured wasps called "ichneumons," which are parasitic on other wasps and on many other insect forms in their larval stages, piercing with a long sharp ovipositor the skin of the unfortunate victim and placing an egg into the defenseless body. The egg will hatch into a small grub which will thereupon begin to feed on the host larva until it is consumed, and then will change into a chrysalis, and finally into a mature ichneumon. These are mostly small, usually shiny black in colour, though some are decorated with brilliant and quite beautiful colours, yellow, red, and orange. But to examine them closely, a hand magnifier is needed – I always carry one in my pocket – and to execute a drawing in any reasonable degree of detail it becomes necessary to render the figure several times larger than life. While these ichneumons prey successfully upon the grubs of larger wasps, their own larvae are similarly parasitized by much smaller ichneumons of the same insect order, illustrating in a very graphic manner Dean Jonathan Swift's famous quatrain:

So naturalists observe, a flea
Hath smaller fleas that on him prey;
And these have smaller still to bite 'em,
And so proceed, ad infinitum!"

Well, not quite "ad infinitum," but researchers have identified at least one series of no fewer than four species of these little wasps that prey on each other "down the line," as it were, presumably maintaining some sort of balance in the food chain of which they form part. I have always been intrigued by the name "ichneumon," as the same word is used for a weasel-like mammal of North Africa. I find that the word, obviously pure Greek, is derived from the Greek verb ἰχνεύειν, meaning "to hunt out." The mammal hunts out and consumes crocodile eggs; the ichneumon wasp hunts out larvae, some of which may be deep in the wood of a living tree.

September 22   Yesterday and today we have been blanketed during the morning hours with a soft coverlet of sea fog, another sure sign of approaching autumn, adding further to the stillness of the surrounding woods. Yesterday, the fog lay under a gray and cloudy sky, and I found myself walking in a gentle rain, not much more than a light distillation of the fog itself, very agreeable on the face as I strode along. But today, the sky above the fog layer is blue and

WESTERN RED CEDAR
Thuja plicata
(fruit cones)

SHORE PINE
Pinus contorta contorta

PLATE XXXIII

clear, and a brilliant sun will no doubt soon burn off the fog and give us another fine autumn day. But the condensing moisture has revealed a great number of perfectly crafted spider webs among the branches of the evergreens, each, so far, unspoiled by breeze or other disturbing movement, each outlined beautifully by a myriad of water droplets, and each containing, in its exact centre, a motionless watchful spider. Because of the morning chill, no flying insects are yet on the wing, to get themselves trapped in the great webs, but sunshine and warmth will not be long on the way, and Mrs. Spider is very much "open for business."

Somewhere behind me, as I paused for a few moments at the corner of the park, a Douglas Squirrel was chittering at me, evidently considering even my quiet harmless presence an unwarrantable invasion of his territory. But this is his time for gathering together his little hoard of food against the oncoming winter. There is probably, in this favoured area, no time in the year when a squirrel would be unable to find an adequate supply of his kind of food, but built-in habits and instincts are strong, so this frisky little mammal busies himself by cutting off the shaggy seed-cones of the Douglas Firs, dropping them to the ground around the tree, then descending and gathering the hoard into his underground winter quarters. He is king of the castle here, for the big Gray Squirrel, which has invaded parks and urban woods in so many areas, displacing almost completely the smaller Red and Douglas Squirrels, has not so far appeared in McKechnie Park.

September 29 Yesterday we had what could be described as an equinoctial storm, the first of the season, causing an abrupt change of weather, with thunder, a brief heavy downpour of rain, and hail adding to the excitement, followed by a rapid clearing of the sky and a sharp lowering of the temperature. This morning the sky is crystal clear, but it is cool and brisk enough to be conducive to vigorous walking. The roadside flowers are practically all gone, only a few yellow blossoms remaining among the masses of fluffy white seed-heads on the Cats-ear dandelions, now tall and straggly. The wayside borders and ditches have an unkempt, end-of-summer look which the bright weather does little to alleviate, though here and there a Scotch Broom is making a valiant attempt at a second blooming.

But the tall, stately conifers seem as fresh and beautiful as ever. Last week, during the morning fog, they appeared misty and ethereal as their shadowy outlines receded in distance, an aspect of a foggy day which always greatly appeals to me; but this morning, the low early sun was striking only the tops of the taller trees, causing them to glow golden-green against the turquoise sky. Many of the red cedars are displaying dense masses of the small olive-green seed-cones, upturned on the downward-drooping leaf-branches (*Plate 33*). The Douglas Firs and the Western Hemlocks also appear both to be carrying large loads of cones.

Here and there along my normal walking routes, I pass an occasional Shore Pine, a much smaller conifer than the other West Coast giants, one of the only two pines native to this coastal area. Scientifically it is known as *Pinus contorta*, from the somewhat twisted and gnarled shape it assumes when grown along the granite-buttressed shoreline, exposed to the ocean winds. But most of the Shore Pines along the more sheltered and better-cultivated route of my walk up the mountainside have relatively straight trunks, while a variety of this same species which grows in the interior of the province is known as *Pinus contorta*, variety *latifolia* (broad-leaved), the Lodgepole Pine. Poles for lodges are not "contorted," and the Lodgepole Pine is a tall straight tree—though how a tree whose foliage consists exclusively of long slender pine needles, two to a tuft, can be characterized as "broad-leaved" tends to elude me. It seems that in reality, the twisted shore-growing trees constitute the more "unusual" variety of a species which normally stands straight and tall, but as it was the variety first classified and named, the title "contorta" has persisted, even for the tall straight Lodgepole Pines of the Interior. One of the quaint peculiarities of plant taxonomy!

The other pine reputed to be indigenous to this coastal region, the Western White Pine, *P. monticola*, a five-needled species, seems to be rare or entirely absent from this immediate area. I have not seen a single specimen along the routes of my daily journeyings, and the Vancouver Natural History Society, in its well-researched book *Nature West Coast*, does not record it from its study area, our nearby Lighthouse Park.

HAIR (OR HARBOUR) SEAL
Phoca vitulina

DOUGLAS SQUIRREL
Tamiasciurus douglasi

WINTER MOTH
Triphosa dubitata

PLATE XXXIV

October

Last night it was full moon, and in consequence there is today a large tide running. It was at about half-ebb as I made my way along the newly-washed beach, a flat-calm sea lapping gently in the morning sunshine. I was about to cross the creek by the still-negotiable causeway of stepping stones, when I was saddened and shocked to come upon the dead body of a Harbour or Hair Seal, lying outstretched upon the sand where the receding tide had deposited it (*Plate 34*). Saddened, because of the empathy I feel for most living things; shocked, because upon closer examination I discovered a neat bullet-hole through the creature's small round head. A fine shot, if you happen to admire clean precise marksmanship. But why? I suppose a fisherman's facile answer might be, "Well, y'know, they do tend to eat up all the fish!" The seals of course do not "eat up all the fish," though fish are a staple of their diets, and they eat what they need to sustain a vigorously active life style. And it must be admitted, when the salmon run is "on" they often tend to gorge. But it is the fishermen themselves who seem to feel they have a prior claim to "all the fish," begrudging any to wild creatures to whom it is their natural diets. We seem to be beset on every hand by selfish greed.

This particular seal was a youngster, between three and four feet in length, and it had not been long dead, for the soft silvery-gray fur, blotched and marbled with a darker gray-brown, was in perfect condition, and the crows had not yet come to call. In order to make a sketch I moved the poor little carcass into a position approximating the attitude it might have adopted had it been alive and basking upon the sand; and, as I did so, the intelligent, dog-like face, with its wide-open though sightless eyes seemed to regard me, even in death, with an expression of sorrowful reproach. The incident rather spoiled, for me, an otherwise golden morning.

Accompanying the conclave of gulls around the outflow of the creek, there is now a small flotilla—twenty or more—of Mallard ducks, of which the gulls and the attendant crows seem to be taking no particular notice, though they are, presumably, contenders for the same general food supply. These ducks are, no doubt, the vanguard of the very large assembly, sometimes running into hundreds, of winter ducks, of several species, who will, as usual, arrive to spend the blustery months in the sheltered waters of this Sandy Cove area.

October 8   Yesterday a change of weather brought a southeast gale, rollers pounding the beach, great trees swaying majestically in the wind, and a heavy downpour of rain that continued all through the night. This morning the sky looks unsettled but very picturesque, big billowy white clouds with gray bases scudding angrily across the heavens. Cypress Creek is a raging river with great volumes of silty water gushing out into the sea. The excitement seems to have infected the gulls and crows, which are even more talkative than usual.

This appears to be the time when the Red Cedars divest themselves of their spent leaves, which for some time now have been hanging rather prettily, cinnamon-brown in colour, among the newer green growth of these great conifers. Each dead twig, with its flat display of withered leaves, is loosely attached to the axil of a recently-formed new twig, and detaches itself at the proper moment to fall silently to the ground. But last night's wind and rain has brought them down in great quantity, and the area around the cedar-trees, including the two large ones outside my front door, is thickly carpeted with a soft brown layer of the fallen twigs – very pleasant to walk upon, but messy to clean up when putting our garden to bed for the winter.

But today the weather is conducive to indoor pursuits, pleasant hours at the drawing board with paper, pencils, water colours, and brushes. Today also, my Constant Companion and I are celebrating fifty-four happy years of constancy and companionship, and an evening by a fire of fragrant alder-logs and a bottle of good wine will provide a good environment in which to await the return of good weather which is promised for tomorrow.

October 12   The clear sunny weather has returned, to provide us with a sort of "Indian Summer" of bright warm afternoons; but the early morning hours have been characterized by more or less dense patches of sea fog which from time to time blow in to shore, reducing visibility almost to zero, then burning off in the strengthening sun, to a day of great brilliance.

The fall of the leaf is well under way, though this is noticeably a slower, more gradual process in this coastal area than in the Interior, or in Eastern Canada. People who, after many years of life in Ontario or Quebec, come to live on these Pacific shores, sometimes say that they miss quite sadly the sudden explosion of brilliant colour which marks the month of October in those more easterly regions. We ourselves felt this deprivation for our first few autumns in the west, but in twenty-five years of Pacific coast living, we have come to love the soft bronze tones, shading into brilliant yellow-gold, which chiefly constitute our autumn tints, accented here and there with the bright vermilion of the Vine Maple, all against the inevitable sombre dark-green back drop of the eternal conifers. Below us on Marine Drive, and handsomely visible from our patio, there is a Broad-leafed Maple, currently in the full glory of autumn colour. When the early morning sun strikes it these mornings, it becomes a torch of flaming gold, changing to a more ruddy gold in the rays of the westering sun as the day dies.

My Constant Companion has frequently remarked that, upon close examination, it is seldom one encounters any one of the great leaves of these maples in a state of complete perfection, and my own observations over a longish period confirm that this is true, except for a very short time after the leaves first uncurl and expand from the early spring buds (*Plate 35*). In a very brief time they seem to be vigorously set upon by a large assortment of insects, blights, fungi, and diseases which cause minor disfigurements on the otherwise beautiful green surface, so that it is, in fact, often difficult to find one without small holes, chewed edges, the serpentine tunnellings of leaf-miners, or the various kinds of discoloration produced by fungi. When the leaves begin to take on their autumn tint, these various disfigurements are apt to show up as odd, and often quite decorative patterns within the generally bronze tone of the changing leaf. Yet, when the full sunshine strikes the tree, all these different tones and patterns dissolve into a blaze of gold which is a heartening sight to see.

I have been watching the very striking autumn display of the common Sumac, of which there are a number of handsome shrubs at several points along my uphill route, especially along the strip of rough land bordering the Upper Levels highway, the most elevated part of my usual morning walk (*Plate 36*). They, like the Vine Maples, add the occasional bright accent to the gentler panoply of autumn splendour. The Sumac, a weed-shrub in Eastern Canada, and also to some extent in the British Columbia Interior, thrives mightily in the rocky waste spaces and adds greatly to the general

October 18

BROAD-LEAF MAPLE
Acer macrophyllum

FLOWERING DOGWOOD
Cornus nuttallii

VINE MAPLE
Acer circinatum

PLATE XXXV

SUMAC
Rhus glabra

PLATE XXXVI

fall brilliance throughout the great Canadian Shield country of Northern Ontario and Quebec. Here along the Pacific coast it occurs more sparingly, and moreover, behaves itself well enough so that it is welcomed by many as a decorative shrub for the roadside garden. At this moment it is at its best, the great multiple leaves, with twenty or more pinnate leaflets each, hanging picturesquely from the furry, or velvety, reddish branches. The long-toothed leaflets, vermilion red on their upper surfaces, have a way of twisting slightly as they hang, showing part of the beautiful pink undersurface, ending in a hair-thin tip. The odd conical flower masses, deep red in colour, have now made seed and deepened in colour to purple-brown, but have maintained their general shape which will in all probability persist throughout the coming winter, long after the leaves are fully shed.

October 25 This morning I have been again carried back in memory to early childhood, by the sight of a large Horse Chestnut tree, of which there are several hereabouts, growing by the roadside in local gardens (*Plate 37*). Although they are "foreigners" to this area, they appear to thrive well and grow to a substantial size. The big spreading leaves are now starting to change their colour, and the ground beneath this particular tree was littered with those already fallen, and with the ripe horse chestnuts, showing brown and glossy between the gaping halves of the green husks, split by the impact of the fall. I recall, even as a small boy, being struck by the beauty of the shiny brown nuts—"conkers" as we called them, as they appeared between the snow-white "flesh" of the newly opened husk.

It was our custom to collect the conkers, bore holes in them, and thread them in a row on a length of string; then there was some sort of game which consisted chiefly in swinging our string of conkers at our neighbour's string of conkers in an effort to split as many as possible in the shortest possible time. What were the rules of the game, and what its winning points, I do not now recall. This morning I slipped one or two of the conkers into my pocket, not for the purpose of playing the conkers-on-a-string game, but the more grown-up object of attempting to capture their beauty in a drawing.

The Horse Chestnut is, indeed, a splendid tree, but a Chestnut it is not, in spite of its being, for the purpose of botanical identification so called in stately Latin, *Hippocastanum*. But it is not of the true *Castanus*, or chestnut tribe, and has been classified in a separate genus, *Aesculus*. And in fact, apart from the name and the shiny brown nut, there is no great similarity between the Horse Chestnut and the true, or sweet, Chestnut tree. A short walk from the *Hippocastanum* that engaged my attention this morning there is, in fact, a large Sweet Chestnut — *Castanus dentata* — the only one, as far as I am aware, growing in this immediate area, for it too is not indigenous to this coast, and I find myself wondering how it came to be here, for it is a large, well-matured specimen, with a two-foot-thick trunk. Here too the ground is strewn with fallen leaves and with the ripe chestnuts peeping from the burst husks. But the differences between it and its equine namesake are here clearly apparent. The leaves, which are deeply toothed — hence the specific name *dentata* — spring alternately from the stems, whereas those of the Horse Chestnut, of an entirely different shape, grow in a fan-shaped display of seven from the end of a single stem. The husks which carry the edible sweet chestnuts are covered with a dense mass of fine sharp prickles, while those of the non-edible horse chestnut carry a limited armour of short stout spines. The flowers of the Horse Chestnut, in springtime, occur in a magnificent candelabrum of red or white blossoms; those of the Sweet Chestnut are long, slender, and somewhat un-spectacular green catkins. The two trees do not seem very much alike but, although neither of them properly belongs in this area, they are of great interest to observe and compare.

For some reason, possibly the "foreign" soil in which this particular Sweet Chestnut tree is growing, most of the fallen nuts, peeping from their split husks or lying scattered about the ground, are thin and undeveloped-looking, and I found it difficult to locate one or more fat ripe nuts similar to those which, as a small boy in Surrey, I used to gather in company with my two elder sisters as we scuffled through the fallen leaves on a sunny October day, so many years ago.

October 31

Hallowe'en — the Eve of All Hallows, or All Saints' Day. Traditionally, all manner of spirits, spooks, hobgoblins and poltergeists will be abroad tonight, witches on their birch brooms will ride to their black sabbaths, and a devilish hullabaloo will take place until these ungodly ones are all chivvied back underground by the Saints Triumphant who will rise in bright array, first thing tomorrow morning. All this, no doubt, was taken terribly seriously a century or so ago. But tonight, the streets where by day I take my constitutional, for a short space, will be well populated by pint-sized witches and warlocks collecting goodies from good-natured householders in the quaint "trick-or-treat" tradition that Hallowe'en has now become.

HORSE-CHESTNUTS ("CONKERS")
Aesculus hippocastanum

AMERICAN SWEET CHESTNUT
Castanus dentata

PLATE XXXVII

The roadways this morning provided no evidence of unseen ghostly battles between the forces of good and evil. A great many of the leaves are now fallen in the rain and wind of the last few days, and the characteristic patterns of the bare branches of red alders, bitter cherries, and broad-leaved maples are beginning to become apparent, while the trees which still bear leaves are very attractive in tones of bronze and gold against the unchanging backdrop of the dark evergreens.

CORAL FUNGUS
Clavaria sp.

WHITE INOCYBE
Inocybe geophylla

"SHAGGY MANE"
Coprinus comatus

BRACKET-FUNGUS
Polyporus versicolor
(on fallen stump)

Pholiota adiposa
(on Douglas Fir trunk)

PLATE XXXVIII

November

The insect world has, for the most part, finished its summer's work and either perished or "gone underground." Most of the female wasps – the future queens – have found themselves small hidey-holes in which to hibernate through the long winter months, though a few belated worker-wasps and a number of the yellow-banded hover-flies are still to be seen feeding, somewhat sleepily, on late blossoms of marigolds and other composite flowers. The Winter Moths, however, are beginning to appear in numbers, flitting at dusk in a rather ghostly manner among the leaves of the surrounding shrubbery, usually settling on the underside of a leaf or branch, spread out flat and quite invisible. At night-time they are much attracted to lighted windows, and can often be seen from within, a small triangular shape in muted tones of gray and brown, well contrasted against the outside darkness. Several species are common in this area, among them the ubiquitous "Fall Canker-worm," but all belong to the great family of the Inch-worms, or *Geometers*. The caterpillars of these attractive little moths provide a truly remarkable example of specialized evolutional development. For, while the larvae of virtually all other moth and butterfly families possess ten "pro-legs" or claspers, upon which they travel along at a more or less straightforward gait, maintaining the six true legs – those which will reappear as legs in the mature insect – free for grasping the leaves of the food-plant, those of the *Geometers* have only two pairs of large pro-legs at the extreme hinder end of the body. With these they secure themselves to the twig along which they are making their way, while they stretch their bodies full-length forward and clasp the twig that much further along with the six true legs. This done, they release the rear-end pro-legs and, bending the body up into a tight loop, bring them forward to a position immediately behind the gripping true legs, which they then release and stretch forward again to repeat the quaint manoeuvre. Thus they make their way in a series of loops or "inches" and in consequence are appropriately called "loopers" or inch-worms; or, more scientifically, *Geometers*, i.e. "Earth Measurers."

November 1

The purpose of this strange development seems to be one of protective mimicry, for the little caterpillars are all green or brown in colouring, and when alarmed they have a way of gripping tightly with the pro-legs the twig on which they are walking or feeding and stretching their bodies out tight and rigid at an angle to the twig, when they become virtually indistinguishable from another branching twig, and are sometimes, in consequence, referred to as "Stick caterpillars."

The females of many species of these little winter moths are poor insignificant looking little creatures, flightless, almost completely wingless, and rather resembling drab brown spiders as they emerge from their cocoons and crawl up to the branch tips of their food-plant trees, where the males of their species wait to mate with them. Their sole remaining purpose is then to lay a clutch of eggs and die. During the whole of this brief reproductory manoeuvre they are a "sitting duck" for a host of insectivorous birds. This is doubtless a wise provision of nature, for, even as it is, some of these insects constitute a serious pest situation, and without such natural controls their depredations could be devastating.

November 8   November might well be styled the "mushroom month," for although wild mushrooms and toadstools of many species are to be found in almost all months of the year, the moist ground of late October and November seems to be the most productive of the fruiting bodies of these strange fungoid "plants." During the past week or so, great numbers of a small and very delicate species, ghostly white at first, then changing to a pale beige colour, have appeared in my garden around the base of such acid-loving plants as Camellia, Azalea, and Rhododendron, and I noticed, during my walk this morning that these have appeared quite commonly everywhere in this vicinity. The excellent little handbook of Drs. Bandoni and Sczawinski, *Guide to the Common Mushrooms of British Columbia* tells me that this species is a White Inocybe, and that "its edibility is questionable" (*Plate 38*). I do not elect to put this questionableness to the test, for though many, possibly most, of the common wild mushrooms are indeed edible, even if not always too palatable, (and some are choice) – unfortunately a few of the non-edible ones are very poisonous indeed, and some of these not too easily distinguishable from the edible species. Unless identification is certain, it is perhaps better to buy our mushrooms at the store.

There is, however, a very attractive house along the route of my daily journey, upon whose broad, well-kept lawn, I am occasionally rewarded by the sight of a group of "Shaggy Mane" mushrooms, standing upright and in their early stages like small white marble columns. While I do not make it a practice to trespass upon my neighbours' property, I always feel a considerable temptation to collect them, for the owners appear not to be aware that these particular wild mushrooms are a great delicacy, sliced thin and sautéed in butter, and they just leave them to ripen and then deteriorate into the black evil-looking inky mass which the Shaggy Mane becomes at its demise.

It has often occurred to me to wonder whether the "manna" which according to the Old Testament story was miraculously provided as food for the Israelites during their wanderings, might not in fact have been some form of wild fungus of an edible nature. "The form of it was like unto the coriander-seed, white," and I am reminded of the pure white flesh of certain of the tiny button-mushrooms when they first appear. The manna was said to have appeared suddenly in the morning as the dew lifted, and I never fail to be surprised at the suddenness with which wild mushrooms seem to appear, especially after a rain. The Israelites were warned not to eat the manna after the sun had been at it and it had started to become putrid and wormy. And I think of the somewhat revolting appearance of some wild mushrooms when they start to disintegrate and are set upon by armies of maggots. I wonder. Some of the "explanations" of the manna given in the concordance attached to my lovely old Family Bible are a good deal less plausible.

Some of the stumps of fallen trees in McKechnie Park are decorated with the large woody masses of the Polypores, or Bracket-funguses, some of which are banded in a series of beautiful colours, from ochre to deep brown, and here and there I notice a clump of Orange-brown mushrooms of the species *Pholiota adiposa*, growing on the trunk of a Douglas Fir, whose days are doubtless numbered. I must assume that the fat, well-rounded form of this particular mushroom, in its early stage of growth, is responsible for the specific name "adiposa"!

The variety of forms and shapes which these various genera of wild fungi assume seems well-nigh infinite, and many do not even approach the commonly-conceived "mushroom" shape. On my return journey this morning, a short distance from my house, I came upon a small growth of white Coral Fungus, resembling a miniature white bush, only an inch or so high, and in fact still more closely resembling a piece of the white south-sea coral one sometimes sees in curio shops—until one handles it, when its rubbery texture at once reveals its mushroom affinity. I brought it in to make a drawing, but hardly had executed the somewhat complex, branched outline before it began to wither and lose its colour and characteristic texture.

Mushrooms gone beyond their prime generally present an unattractive and unappetizing spectacle. They look poisonous, even when they aren't, and have led to all sorts of grisly folk legend. One forms an arresting mental picture of the unspeakable Aggripina dishing up a brew of the "Destroying Angel" mushroom for the domestically inept though administratively able Emperor Claudius, in the sick Roman year of A.D. 54. And the late H.G. Wells, that incomparable writer of short stories, in "The Purple Pileus" tells with rare humour of an inoffensive little man who, thinking to commit suicide by eating poisonous-looking wild mushrooms, is sent instead into an insane paroxysm during which he sets things to rights in his own unsympathetic family, to the subsequent great improvement of his own lot. The mushroom which the author of the tale doubtless had in mind was the beautiful, though poisonous Fly Agaric (*Amanita muscaria*), known to be hallucinatory in its effects when eaten by human beings.

November 15   The migratory birds are now all long gone to sunnier climes, and the regular winter population now have it all their own way. In the graceful, departed days of ocean travel, about twenty minutes before the lines were cast off and the tug boats started to inch us away from the quay, the voices of the deck stewards, well raised above the general hubbub, could be heard calling "All ashore as is goin' ashore!" and the seeing-off parties of relatives and friends would be seen streaming down the gang plank until all were gone. The great vessel would move slowly out into the harbour and her own engines would begin to throb. Then we would all settle down into our normal ship-board routine as we got under way and took our first meal on board. With the winter birds, the opposite procedure seems to hold—"All south as is goin' south!" pipes some cocky little winter sparrow, in my imagination, and all are now away, leaving the available feed to the Chickadees, Juncos, Towhees, and House-finches who will be with us all winter long (*Plate 39*).

The bird feeder which hangs outside our kitchen window is a busy port of call and is an unfailing source of amusement to us. My Constant Companion conjures up imaginary thought-processes for

BLACK-CAPPED CHICKADEES
Parus atricapillus

OREGON JUNCOS
Junco oregonis

RUFOUS-SIDED TOWHEE
Pipilo erythopthalmus

PLATE XXXIX

the various birds that come to feed, as small dramas appear to develop out there among the bird seed: the Oregon juncos, which come in flocks but seem polite little birds and await their turn among the branches of the nearby dogwood tree; the Black-capped Chickadees, also arriving in flocks but staying only a second or two as they pick off two or three grains of seed, then away in a flash of black-and-white tail feathers; the Towhee, who hunkers down right in the middle of the heap of seed and eats all around him, rather like a storybook miser gloating over his hoard, to the quite evident irritation of the other species. But my ornithological friends tell me that, due to the extremely rapid metabolic rate of these small birds, many species must eat close to their own weight of food each day in order to keep their vigorous life style going, and that, after a long winter's night, they must, first thing in the morning find a source of food to revive them. Certainly our bird feeder presents a Grand Central Station aspect shortly after daybreak each morning, and my feathered friends seem likely to keep me poor buying the mixed seed which I supply to them.

Actually, in this area of relatively mild winters there is usually no serious lack of natural food to be found for insectivorous and seed-eating birds, though they doubtless have to work a little harder for it than in the halcyon days of summer. But when we do experience a "cold snap," or during the infrequent periods when the ground is covered with snow, the small birds suffer and the good citizens' bird feeders become popular – and vital – gathering places.

November 20　　We are now in the midst of just such a cold snap as I have referred to in connection with my feathered neighbours and their winter troubles. The weather today is beautifully clear and sunny, but the temperature has dropped well below the freezing point and as I set out this morning there was, over everything, a heavy coating of white hoar-frost. The fallen leaves, lying thick upon the ground, were each outlined in silvery white, accenting the characteristic shape of each species in a very beautiful manner. The grassy verges of the roadway were picturesquely frosted, and hard and crunchy to walk on. A very pleasant morning.

I made my way as far as possible along the shore, but Cypress Creek is now far too swollen for any sensible attempt to cross, and I was obliged to clamber back across the drift logs, now also coated with hoar-frost, and extremely slippery and dangerous, so that I was constrained to proceed with considerable caution, feeling I was courting the danger of slipping down between the great logs and breaking a leg. I was relieved to arrive safely on the landward side of the beach.

Several species of ducks were swimming and diving for food along the water's edge, apparently undeterred by the cold weather, Mallards, Widgeons, and Surf-scoters (*Plate 40*). I sometimes find myself wondering how they can endure this life in the cold water, but they are of course designed and built for it, with their high normal body temperature and the incredibly efficient insulating system provided by their down-and-feather plumage. The sea water does not, in fact, vary in temperature more than a degree or two between summer and winter, whatever the seasonal variations in weather and air temperature may be. A little further out from the shore, several pairs of Western Grebes were swimming and diving, easily distinguished by their long, graceful necks. Still further from shore a long floating tree trunk, probably broken away from some log boom, was moving steadily westward on the ebbing tide, with four deck-passengers on board, two white seagulls and two black, long-necked cormorants. And, to complete the pageant, perhaps half a mile from the shore – though they seem closer – two great ships are lying at anchor, awaiting berths in our labour-troubled inner harbour, beyond the Lions Gate bridge. The high atmospheric pressure which has brought us the fine clear weather and the cold, brisk day, has also resulted in an almost flat calm; and the difference in temperature between the air and the sea water has produced a light surface-mist, which gives the big, silent vessels a somewhat ethereal appearance, as though they were not quite of this world.

The clear cold weather persisted for several delightful days, but yesterday, as the professional meteorologists put it, "a low-pressure front moved in from the Pacific," bringing with it dark lowering clouds, and overnight a deluge of rain which has brought down the last few lingering leaves from the deciduous trees, and imparted a glossy, washed appearance to evergreen shrubs like the holly, ivy, salal, and particularly the camellias in our garden, which are thick with next year's flower-buds, the leaves gleaming and polished in the morning light. The big sword-ferns, too, look green and happy, though the bracken, which does not survive the winter, now displays dead fronds of golden brown, still retaining their graceful outline. Some of the smaller shrubs of the Ocean Spray have also retained a small residue of their odd-shaped leaves, which have

November 25

Surf Scoter
Melanitta perspicillata

Western Grebe
Aechmophorus occidentalis

Plate XL

taken on a rich turkey-red colour, and give a touch of late brilliance to an otherwise rather drab and dull winter environment.

As I passed on my way this morning two Japanese gardeners were working on the shrubbery in a nearby property, apparently moving a small tree to a new location. They are very expert, and seem capable of intense concentration on what they are doing. They do not look up or pause in their work as I pass, but this morning I gave them a cheery "Ohaio, gozai-masu!" which did cause them to look around in surprise and reward me with a toothy Japanese smile, though from their chuckles I would gather they considered my attempt at Japanese not very successful and my pronunciation appalling! But, when one can courteously do so, it is rewarding to watch these Japanese gardeners at work. We have seen them, in Southern Japan, tending the pine trees in parks and hotel grounds, seeming to give close professional attention to individual twigs to produce the condition of beauty and health they desire.

December

December 5   The winter solstice approaches, and the mornings are dark. When I set out this morning the sun, well to the south of east, had climbed only a few degrees into a flaming morning sky, throwing into silhouetted outline the tall buildings of Vancouver City, and far behind them the sharp conical shape of Mount Baker, seventy miles away as the crow flies. This splendid eleven-thousand foot mountain, the most northerly of the long line of volcanoes that form the Cascade Range, is not "extinct" but merely dormant, and displays its sleeping activity by a number of small fumaroles that spout steam and sulphureous vapours out of the lofty crater. Local Indian legend informs us that Mount Baker did, in fact, erupt about three hundred years ago, a fact which had been generally regarded as a pleasant curiosity until, last year, Mount St. Helen's, a very similar volcano a few hundred miles south in the same range, blew out its entire side with serious loss of life and great devastation. Glances at Mount Baker, like mine this morning, have become noticeably more speculative.

But I did not allow these musings unduly to depress me as I walked on down to the beach, where I encountered my good friend Gordon Tallman, busily at work obtaining his Yule-log for the approaching Christmas festivities. With a large steel wedge and a hardwood follower, Gordon was proceeding to split lengthwise, by blows from a heavy sledge hammer, a three-foot length of tree trunk selected from the surrounding mass of stranded drift wood. Gordon, himself a nature lover, drew my attention to an eagle which had been perched at the top of a nearby fir tree, apparently watching him work. There is that about the eagle eye which gives the impression of minute scrutiny. As I moved on down the beach, the eagle also took flight and went flapping majestically along the shore toward Lighthouse Park, where it appears to have a mate. It was not, this time, mobbed by a group of noisy crows, as is so often the case, but, as it passed overhead, a very large flock of small birds rose from the seaweed-covered boulders where they had been foraging, and wheeled in a wide circle before settling again a little further along the shore. These I took to be starlings, but I was unable to detect the prominent and beautiful speckled markings I associate with starlings in the winter time. Cowbirds? But the brown-headed cowbird is not a winter species here, nor does it, as far as I am aware, congregate in large flocks like the starling. Starlings, indeed they must have been, which is a pity, for though these hardy immigrants have spread themselves continent-wide and are a great pest in many areas, hitherto they have not been particularly numerous in the forested North Shore area.

Occasionally during my morning forays, especially when I take the low level route which includes a stretch along the beach, I find myself confronted with signs of small tragedies which are difficult of ready explanation – outside the usual comings and goings of the normal web of life. *December 10*

This morning, a short distance along the high-tide line, I came across a dead dogfish – or, rather, half a dead dogfish, for the creature, a small shark, had been cut or bitten neatly in two, and only the front portion with its gill-slits and its ugly gaping slot of a mouth was present. Could it have been sliced in two by a boat's propeller? Not too likely, for the line of severance was too clean. Or, possibly, bitten in two by a seal? Perhaps a little more probable.

Further along, I was surprised to find the whole body of a dead salmon, and I was led to wonder anew at this very unlikely circumstance. It occurred to me that this unhappy fish might have been caught by, and then dropped by, one of the eagles which inhabit our area and are often to be seen patrolling the shore from high above. But eagles do not often drop their prey, once the great talons have sunk in and locked.

Both the salmon and the dogfish (except for its hind end) were bodily intact except for the eyes, all of which were missing, doubtless pecked out of the dead bodies by the crows. This predilection for eyes, apparently regarded as choice tidbits by many predators, has often been remarked upon by students of animal behaviour.

Last night brought us a great storm, with a mighty wind roaring all night in the trees – the big Douglas Firs that surround my house swaying alarmingly in the uproar. The roadway along my route this morning was liberally strewn with green branches tossed hither and yon in the tempest, and during the night hours one enormous limb broke from its high place to strike the corner of the house as it fell, shaking the building alarmingly, but, fortunately causing no *December 16* important damage. It is rather strange that although the timber of the Douglas Fir is among the toughest and strongest, internationally in demand as construction material, yet the limbs and branches during the period of growth seem unusually brittle, and many become casualties during a serious wind storm.

My intention this morning was to follow my low-level route along the shore, but I was soon confronted with a scene of disaster. Although the wind was rapidly abating, a mountainous surf was pounding the beach and, coupled with an unusually high tide – last night was "new moon" – the sea was invading the residential properties along the shore front, and the good citizens were frantically at work rescuing their belongings from flooded basements and gardens.

When my Constant Companion and I, twenty years ago, first came to live in West Vancouver and were looking for a home, we – and especially I myself – were very much hoping to find an available house with a garden fronting directly on the beach. This morning was only the last of several occasions on which we have had reason to congratulate ourselves that we were unsuccessful, and settled instead for a property overlooking the sea but a hundred and twenty feet above it, on a solid, solid rock!

Cypress Creek is again a raging torrent, from the heavy rain that accompanied the gale, and at its outflow on to the beach, where I so often sit on a drift log watching the sea gulls arguing with the crows, a great battle was in progress between the roaring flow of fresh water from the creek and the wild surf opposing it. The gulls and crows were wheeling excitedly for there was now no shingly beach exposed, on which to forage for food. But, as I now sit writing, later in the day, the storm is past and the sea calm except for a certain remaining swell, but the period of high tides has yet to pass and the unfortunate people along the shore will, many of them I fear, have to put up with a rather messy, smelly house in which to spend Christmas.

> Except an house be founded on a rock,
> Their labour is but lost that build it!

December 21   The Holly and the Ivy, when they are both full-grown,
                      Of all the trees that are in the wood, the Holly bears the crown!

Although neither of these celebrated evergreen plants is native to this area, both were introduced – perhaps by homesick British

"The Holly"
Ilex aquifolium

"And The Ivy"
Hedera helix

Plate XLI

settlers—many years ago, and both have acclimatized themselves and have flourished exceedingly (*Plate 41*). Thick carpets of ivy appear at the foot of gardens at many points along the route of my walk, and many of the big Douglas Fir trunks are encircled by its thick cable-like stems and enshrouded by the glossy five-angled leaves, for the ivy is epiphytic in its habit.

And where the local property owners have been careful enough—and knowledgeable enough—to plant both a male holly tree and a female one in reasonably close proximity to one another, the latter is displaying, at this season of the year, a crop of bright berries to help in enlivening the generally dull appearance of the winter landscape.

One is inclined to wonder why the holly "bears the crown," or for that matter, why a crown should be involved at all. Undoubtedly this must be on account of the deep religious significance which has been attached to the holly plant from remote historical times. Certainly, the holly figured in the pagan observances both of the Druids and of the early Romans. The word "holly" is undoubtedly just another form of "holy" and the plant itself at some point became confused with the Holm-oak or Holy-oak (*Quercus ilex*) of the Romans, and the specific name, *Ilex*, of this oak has been adopted as a generic name, *Ilex*, for the holly tree. Be that as it may, the holly and the ivy figure conspicuously in the design of Christmas greeting cards, and no house can consider itself adequately decorated for the Christmas festivities unless holly and ivy are somewhere in evidence.

Indeed, it is to me one of the intriguing aspects of Christmas, as it is now celebrated in Christian countries, that so much from the ancient pagan rites attached to the winter solstice have become intermingled with the touching human story, told with such artless simplicity in the Gospels, of the nativity at Bethlehem, resulting in a festival that no one can resist in its heart-stopping beauty. In the Christmas Carol whose opening couplet I quoted at the head of this entry, each verse relates some pagan aspect of the holly, then finishes with the simple statement, rather like a diary-entry, "And Mary bore sweet Jesus Christ in the Crowning of the Year"! What could be more lovely?

December 25   The spirit of Christmas casts its spell over this local community as it does upon every town, city, and country throughout the Christian world, and indeed in many parts of the globe where Christian light does not too brightly shine, but where human fellow-feeling and brother-love still illuminate the hearts of men. As I took my walk this bright chilly morning, the world seemed, in some strange, inexplicable way, a different place because it is Christmas morning. Christmas is, for sure, far, far more than a season of feasting, of frantic shopping, of sending greetings and of giving and receiving gifts. As I strode along on my familiar way, the magic seemed to seep through the holly-wreathed front doors and out into the street, a warm hint of cosiness within, of joyful homecomings, of sparkling-eyed children, of hearts of the more fortunate opened in a genuine concern for those less lucky. Truly, the Christmas message, and the blessed event of which it is a memorial, are a gift from heaven above.

For many years, my Constant Companion and I have made it our custom to hold "open house" from early in the evening of Christmas Eve. At one point in our wedded pilgrimage we found ourselves disenchanted with the frantic rush of "preparations for the Feast," lasting up to, and even beyond, the magic midnight hour. This, we felt, deflected our attention and that of many of our friends from the full appreciation of the Yuletide mystique, of which midnight, Christmas Eve is the focal point. From that day on we have made sure, each year, that all the elaborate preparations for the great day have been completed by mid-afternoon on Christmas Eve, and year by year an increasing number of our friends and neighbours, like-minded, have arrived for an evening by the fireside. To light, with due ceremony, the huge Yule-log, specially cut for us some days previously by Gordon Tallman, brought in by his three tall sons, regular participants, and kindled from the charred remains of the previous year's Yule-log, to impart a modicum of symbolic continuity to the custom. To pledge one another in hot Wassail – in one of its many forms, in our case hot spiced cider well laced with brandy – served in goblets from a great bowl brought in from the kitchen to the singing of the ancient Wassail-song and set down steaming before the blazing Yule-log. To engage in merry chatter, and to sing Christmas carols, often in quite good harmony, with one or other of our musical friends at the piano. And, at or about eleven thirty, one by one quietly to depart, most to attend a midnight service or Mass at their several local churches. And when the last guest has left, ourselves to sit quietly by the dying fire "to hear" (as we say) "the angels flap their wings" and to give thanks in our hearts for the blessed quiet of this magical hour of the year's most lovely season.

December 31 And so the year has gone full circle. The cycle of life of green and growing things has returned to where we started, with tight, shiny new catkins on the Red Alders, the strange flat flower-buds already taking shape on the Flowering Dogwoods, and tiny green spikes of snowdrops and even crocuses already visible in more sunny and sheltered corners of the neighbours' gardens, as well as our own. The myriads of twigs on the leafless alder-spinneys are once more a gray misty cloud against the somber fir-clad mountainside. Once again, this morning, I spotted one of the eagles soaring over the Pacific Environmental Laboratory below us, where the big round tanks of experimental fish doubtless frustrate the great bird, for the tops of the tanks are protected with wire netting. The shore birds along the beach are present in numbers, and the small feathered folk are busy on the feeder hanging outside our kitchen window, all reminding us of the continuity of the great web of life.

This evening we shall once again sit by the fire and watch the old year a-dying and the new one a-borning. With thankful hearts we shall again pledge one another in a glass of the ruby fluid and acknowledge, without rancour, that the world, like the Dumb Walking Man and his Constant Companion, is one year older.

Index